CHASING EXCELLENCE

A STORY ABOUT BUILDING
THE WORLD'S FITTEST ATHLETES

CHASING EXCELLENCE

★

BEN BERGERON

FOREWORD BY KATRÍN DAVÍÐSDÓTTIR

TWO-TIME WORLD'S FITTEST WOMAN

LIONCREST
PUBLISHING

CHASING EXCELLENCE

A Story about Building the World's Fittest Athletes

ISBN   978-1-61961-727-8 *Hardcover*

978-1-61961-728-5 *Paperback*

978-1-61961-729-2 *Ebook*

CONTENTS

FOREWORD... 9

INTRODUCTION 21

1. COMMITMENT 33

2. GRIT 47

3. POSITIVITY 61

4. EMBRACE ADVERSITY 71

5. CONFIDENCE 87

6. MAXIMIZING MINUTES 105

7. THE PROCESS 121

8. CONTROL 137

9. TURN THE PAGE 149

10. HUMILITY... 159

11. COMPETITIVE EXCELLENCE 171

12. CLUTCH 181

EPILOGUE...193

ABOUT THE AUTHOR............................... 199

FOREWORD

★

MAY 23, 2014

COPENHAGEN, DENMARK

Though it's hard to imagine now, there was a time when Ben Bergeron was not my coach.

In 2014, during the CrossFit Games Europe Regional, I didn't have a coach at all. I had been to the Games twice before. I stand on the starting mat waiting for Event 5 to start, and I'm poised to return for a third time. I'm sitting in first place overall, but I don't feel like it. As I stare at the ropes dangling at the far end of the competition floor, an overwhelming sense of dread washes over me. This is *the* event—the one that will make or break my chances.

Event 5 is ten legless rope climbs, for time. That's it. Nowhere to hide. I'm strong and fit, and confident about all of the Regional events—except this one. Rope climbs have always been hard for me. When I practiced this one at home, I didn't finish in the eleven-minute time cap. Then, to my dismay, I watched as most of the women in the previous three heats before mine finished easily. I've done the math—if I don't finish this event, I'm not going to qualify for the CrossFit Games this year.

As I stand on the starting mat, my stomach is in knots.

The buzzer goes off, and I momentarily forget my fear as the adrenaline starts rushing and I run toward my rope. I do a rope climb and *woah!*—I feel like I'm flying! I feel great! I jump back up sooner than I thought I would be able to and I do another one. So far so good—I'm moving way faster than I thought I would. I finish my third and fourth climbs and, wow, maybe I will just do so good in this event!

And then it hits me. During the fifth climb, I feel the pull in my biceps and the grip in my forearms start to fade. I make it up, but I have to kip harder and take smaller pulls. By round six I know I am in trouble—the sixth climb takes everything I have. I'm having to rest more and more between each climb, which only fuels my growing sense of panic; I look around at the other athletes and see that everyone is still moving continuously through the workout. I know I need more rest, but I can't stop. *I'm going to fall too far behind.*

I didn't know it, but the seventh climb would change the course of my entire life.

I make it almost all the way up—I'm no more than a foot away. Everything is burning, but I have to make it to the top. Each rope climb is so valuable. I can't fail this one. I'm so close—all I have to do is let go with one hand and touch the crossbeam. I can feel that it's not there, but I have to try. It has to be there. *Please be there.* I let go and reach with everything I have, but I don't make it. I slide down the whole rope, the palms on both my hands burning with heat, the sides of my fingers blistering.

I fall to my knees and bury my face in my hands and start crying, right there on the competition floor. There's still more than three minutes left in the event, but I feel as if I've already failed. My head is everywhere. I know that if don't make this climb and finish the event, I'll slip out of qualifying position for the CrossFit Games. The thought is so devastating, it feels like it's already happened. I know by now that I'm not going to make it, and I'm shattered. I give up. After the event, I drop from first on the leaderboard down to sixth—out of contention for the CrossFit Games.

Ben Bergeron wasn't my coach at the time, but I had worked with him a few times, and we were friends. After I missed qualifying for the Games, I got a text from him. "I know you might not see this right now, but this could be the best thing that ever happened to you." The best thing that ever happened to me?! I was so mad at him. How could he say that about something I was so devastated about? It took me a week to respond to his text. We laugh at it now...because he was right.

After Regionals, I had had a lot of time for self-reflection. It might have looked like I missed the Games because I failed physically. But I knew that was only part of the story. Yes, my legless rope climbs needed work. But so did my mind. Later that year, I started working with Ben as my full-time coach. I moved from Iceland to Boston to train with him at his gym, CrossFit New England (CFNE).

At first, adopting Ben's concepts was like learning to write with my left hand. His approach to everything was unlike anything I had ever experienced. CFNE was a gym, but it felt more like an Ivy League university. One time, after a particularly frustrating training session, I ripped off my lifting belt, threw it at a wall, and stormed outside. Ben gave me a minute, then followed me out there. With his usual stoic calm, he came up to me and said, "We don't do that here." I immediately realized that he was right—that's not how we carry ourselves here.

That's the way it is with Ben. He focuses on developing character, because he believes that better people make better athletes. In those early months, we talked about things like positivity and controlling how I reacted to any given event, whether it was failing a squat clean or spilling coffee in my car. I saw how much he loved and cared about his family, his friends, and the members of his gym. By just being around him, I learned how to believe in myself while keeping both feet on the ground. Ben talked about mindset constantly—before workouts, after workouts, and sometimes during workouts. He taught me what to focus on, and what to ignore. I was living with his family at the time, so we talked about mindset outside the gym too—in the car, at the dinner table, everywhere.

Over time, it started to sink in. I was getting fitter every day, but the real growth was happening between my ears. We did thrusters and pull-ups and *lots* of rope climbs, but what we really focused on was mindset. Because of Ben, I was becoming a better person. It was subtle at first, but over time it became impossible to overlook—the more I grew characteristically, the better I became as an athlete.

It's impossible to spend any time around Ben without becoming a better person. Other than my grandfather, there is no one I know who lives with more integrity. Ben always does the right thing. He knows what is most important to him, and he has an inflexible set of core values that he lives, breathes, and teaches to others. It's one of the first things you notice when you walk into CrossFit New England—the way everyone watches Ben. When he talks, all eyes are on him. The athletes, competitors, and regular members alike hang on his every word. Without demanding it, he has the full attention of the room.

People look up to and follow Ben because of the personal example he sets. He works harder, longer, and smarter and is more dedicated, passionate, detail-oriented, and enthusiastic than anyone I have ever met. He lives in constant pursuit of excellence and leads by example every second of every day.

From the very beginning, Ben's standards for excellence have made me want to work harder. I know I'm not the only one; I think anyone who has come to train with Ben has had the realization: "Wow, okay, so *that* is what hard work is." I thought I knew what hard work was before, but Ben taught me the difference between putting a lot of work into something and giving *everything I have* into something.

He does this in a very subtle, quiet way. Ben never says much. He picks his words very carefully, so if you ever get a "nice work," or a "well done," you know you did something special. What makes Ben so unique is that he manages to bring out your best without any pressure. "No pressure" sounds easy, but it's anything but—being your best demands everything you are capable of, and everything you are capable of is *hard*. Ben never expects me, or any other athlete, to do more than we are capable of, but he *always* expects us to give everything we have. That's what got me hooked in the beginning. It was the challenge to constantly deliver the best I was capable of, every single time.

The process is something that Ben puts a lot of emphasis on, and he pays more attention to the effort I put in than how much I lifted or how fast I went. It was during that first year of training with him that I fell in love with the process. I responded to Ben's ideas, his enthusiasm, his energy. I began to relish the challenge of waking up every day and becoming better. Though I moved halfway around the world with the goal of making it back to the CrossFit Games, Ben and I never actually talked about the Games. We didn't talk about qualifying, we didn't talk about finishing in the top ten, and we certainly didn't talk about winning. What we did talk about was giving full effort in every single moment of every single day, and becoming the best we could possibly be.

I remember the first time I truly understood what that meant.

It was during the 2015 CrossFit Games, right before a rope-climb event—an event that was my weakness, the one that had kept me from making it to the Games the previous year. I was nervous; I knew the other competitors could go faster than me. I had been doing well in the events leading up to that workout—so well, in fact, that I found myself sitting at the top of the leaderboard. That meant I had to wear the leader jersey. *Of course I am wearing the leader jersey*, I thought. *All eyes will be on me during an event that will just knock me right back down. Perfect.* I started panicking and was in tears in the warm-up area.

In that moment of fear, anxiety, and frustration, I remember saying to Ben, "Please just say something; say anything." He looked at me and told me the leader jersey didn't matter. We don't look at the leaderboard, he said. It's just a meaningless score in the middle of the weekend, and you always give everything you have, regardless of what place you are in. He reminded me how hard we had worked on rope climbs. We really had—we had worked on them almost every single day since they had kept me from competing at the CrossFit Games last year. He reminded me how much they had improved, and he was able to shift my mindset from being nervous about how much faster other girls would be able to go to a mindset of being excited to go out there and show how far we had come with rope climbs. "It's just me and you out there," he said. "It's no different than being back home in the gym." I just had to go out there and do one rope climb, he said. *I can do that*, I thought. "After that first climb, just rest until you feel like you're ready," he said. "Then do one more." That didn't seem so hard. Two rope climbs—that became my goal.

I vividly remember being out on that big soccer field, looking up at the ropes. I did just what Ben said, and felt this sudden confidence come over me. I always had Ben's voice in my head, but now it was coming from the inside, not the outside. I ended up making *three* rope climbs in that event. I still got time-capped, finished in fifteenth place, and lost the leader jersey, but I didn't care. It was the happiest I had been the entire week of the Games—for the first time, I really understood how maximizing my full potential could be a "win," even if it technically wasn't one on the leaderboard. Yes, I was clearly competing against other women in a competition—but within myself, I *wasn't* competing against others. I was competing against my best self. You can't be better than your absolute best.

Winning the 2015 CrossFit Games was a pivotal moment in my relationship with Ben—not because we won the

Games, but because of the way it validated so much of what we believe in and our overall approach to training in general. It's not about the big goals. It's not about the confidence to be able to say them out loud. It's the focus and dedication to the task at hand, no matter how small, and giving your very best in each and every moment. Ben and I talk about it like being on a beach. We don't look at the whole beach; we focus on one grain of sand. We only see one grain at a time, and that grain gets our full attention. After a full day of focusing on a single grain at a time, we leave the beach. That's when we look at it as a whole. That is when we see the beauty of it all and reflect on it.

Other than my grandparents, there is no one in this world who has had more of an impact on me than Ben Bergeron has. There isn't a day that goes by when I don't think about how lucky I am to have ended up in New England with Ben as my coach. I have grown so much as a person because of him, and the character traits he's helped me develop—gratitude, humility, dedication, positivity, poise, focus, resilience, and an eagerness to continuously grow—have less to do with CrossFit than they do with life. Long after my athletic career is over, when my gold medals are dusty and competition is just a memory, I will be, as so many others are, the person I am today because of Ben Bergeron. No matter where life takes me, Ben's lessons will always be part of me. When I have my own family, I hope to pass those lessons on to them.

Ben and his family have become my family, and I can only hope I have done a fraction for them of what they have done for me. I have nothing but the greatest love and admiration for Ben. His friendship, wisdom, and kindness are gifts that I will treasure forever.

—KATRÍN DAVÍÐSDÓTTIR, 2015 & 2016
CROSSFIT GAMES CHAMPION

INTRODUCTION

★

*Gentlemen, we will chase perfection, and
we will chase it relentlessly, knowing all
the while we can never attain it. But along
the way, we shall catch excellence.*

—VINCE LOMBARDI JR.

Once a year, thousands of very peculiar fans descend upon Carson, California's StubHub Center. Most are tanned, tattooed, and brightly clad. They share the same rugged, outdoorsy look, but that's not the main thing they have in common; it's their physiques that mark them as part of a larger tribe. Everyone here is an *athlete*.

Such is the CrossFit Games—home of the fittest fans on Earth.

I'm sitting among them, as one of them, in the stands of StubHub's soccer complex, waiting for Katrín Davíðsdóttir to take the field for Event 8 of the 2016 CrossFit Games—or, as Katrín has been apprehensively putting it all day, "our rope-climb workout." It comes at about the halfway point through the competition, but it might as well be our final exam; it is the biggest physical and mental challenge Katrín is likely to face all week.

Given the choice between coaching an athlete with above-average talent or one who is mentally tough, it might surprise you to hear I'd pick the former. Not because I believe talent is more important, but because I know I can teach someone to be mentally tough. Over the last ten years of coaching athletes to the top of the most grueling sport in the world, I've seen what mental toughness does to talent. I've watched it elevate athletes from the middle of the pack to the podium. The reigning 2016 Fittest Man and Fittest Woman on Earth are both my clients, and they owe their titles to a mindset that was arduously developed. I have coached athletes to six world championships, and have learned that few things make as big an impact as mental toughness.

There is a lot of misunderstanding around what mental toughness is. Because of this, people struggle to practice and improve it. Most people think that mental toughness is something you're born with—like blue eyes or freckles. Nothing could be further from the truth. We can condition our resolve for excellence or weakness, for resiliency or rigidity. At our best, mental toughness can fill the gaps that our talent and our practice have left open. And it can get us to the top of a 20-foot rope when our lungs are burning, our arms are like lead, and the competition is breathing down our neck.

It's a fact I'm counting on heavily as I wait for Katrín's heat to start. The event is called Climbing Snail, and it consists of three rounds of a 500-meter run up the berm of the soccer stadium, two rope climbs, a 40-foot Snail push, followed by two more rope climbs—as CrossFit Games commentator Pat Sherwood has described it, "a wonderful combination of fun, miserable, and unknown."

The unknown is a hallmark of the CrossFit Games. Every year, the Games introduces new events and new equipment that tests the competitors' ability to adapt on the fly. Last year, it was the Pig, a 580-pound, refrigerator-like object that the athletes flipped down the field. The year before that, they sprinted while carrying sandbags with the dimensions of a picnic blanket. This year, it's the Snail—a 400-pound cylinder filled with sand and lined with red padding. The Snail was specifically created for this event at the CrossFit Games—none of the athletes have ever trained with a Snail before, there are no Snails in the warm-up area, and they're not permitted to so much as touch them prior to the start of their heat.

The Snail is the major unknown in this event, but it's not the only one. The climbing ropes are different, too. In almost every gym in the world, ropes run from the ground to the ceiling, but they have been shortened for this event. They dangle five feet above thick red crash pads, like utilitarian streamers. The shortened rope changes the game a bit—instead of performing a traditional rope climb, which most Games athletes can do in their sleep, they will have to perform a legless rope climb before transitioning to using their legs once they get high enough.

This will be harder for all the athletes, but it's particularly daunting for Katrín. Rope climbs have had her number since 2014, when, at a Regional qualifying event, she collapsed on the floor in an emotional meltdown and failed to earn a spot to the Games.

I smile at the memory. As is so often the case, Katrín's darkest hour would prove, in time, to be the best thing that could have happened to her—after missing the CrossFit Games in 2014, she moved to Boston to train with me and ended up surprising everyone by winning the 2015 Games. Since that emotional breakdown in 2014, we have worked tirelessly on her mental toughness (and her upper-body pulling strength) so she would never be in that emotional situation again.

Still, rope climbs are a specter, something to survive. That they've shown up in this event, alongside the unknown Snail, only adds to the uncertainty. Typically, I know how Katrín will perform in a given workout, but this isn't any given workout. The one thing we do know does not provide much comfort—there is huge risk/reward in an event like this. One mistake, especially on a rope climb, can cost upwards of a minute, which, at the Games, can mean the difference between ten and fifteen places.

As I wait for Katrín's heat to start, I'm anxious and excited.

Snails from the previous heat are littered everywhere, like strange Martian hay bales. I'm sitting with Matt O'Keefe, Katrín's agent and one of my closest friends. We watch as a small army of equipment team volunteers struggle to push them all back into place. They're pushing them in teams of two—it's a good reminder of just how superhuman these athletes are. With so many of them everywhere, doing extraordinary things so effortlessly, it's easy to forget.

Finally, the athletes of Heat 2 take the field. Katrín is in lane 13, right in the middle. From where I'm sitting, I can see her expression harden. Her eyebrows furrow; her eyes narrow. Her fingers twitch as she waits for the start. Dave Castro, Director of the CrossFit Games, gives the ten-second cue. Kat leans forward and drops her head.

The starting beep blares, and twenty of the world's fittest women take off down the soccer field to jockey for position on the berm run. The berm is kind of terrible. It's only a 500-meter loop, but it rises and falls over five stories of stadium stairs and steep inclines. "It's just long enough that you start losing hope," Canadian Games competitor Patrick Vellner says later, only half-joking.

There's not much separation after the first run, and all the girls breeze through the first two rope climbs to arrive at the Snail more or less together. From where I'm sitting behind the finish line, it's a bizarre sight—with the women hidden behind them, the twenty red cylinders appear to be rolling down the field on their own. Katrín's second round is conservative; most of the competitors have established a strong lead over the reigning champion. But she's still feeling out the workout and being smart. I unclench my hands slightly. In round three, the final round, she picks up the pace as the other women begin to fade—she passes five people on the final berm run and returns to her rope among the leaders.

Katrín makes quick work of the final two rope climbs, then

jogs her Snail in and takes sixth place overall. She throws both hands in the air and celebrates as though she's won the event. She finished ahead of both of her top rivals, Tia-Clair Toomey and Sara Sigmundsdóttir, which is good for her position on the leaderboard, but that's not why she's thrilled. She's thrilled because her performance was representative of our ethos—she maximized every minute of the event and competed with excellence despite the adversity of unfavorable movements and not being able to physically match her competitors.

This mindset, this dedication to competitive excellence, is what sets Katrín apart in the sport of CrossFit. It's the reason she's the two-time Fittest Woman on Earth. In a sport where differences in physical ability are negligible, Katrín has separated herself with a mental game that is unmatched.

Was she born this way? No. Far from it—just two years ago, Katrín was served a small dose of adversity at Regionals and responded with an emotional breakdown on the competition floor. Before she was a two-time world champion, Katrín was immature, emotional, and weak-minded. The mindset that has propelled her to the top of the podium at the CrossFit Games was a learned behavior.

The mindset of a champion is not some innate character trait that you have or don't have based on DNA, fate, or sheer dumb luck. This is good news for all of us. It means that, through deep and meaningful practice, we can all forge and sharpen the mindset of a champion and deploy it to improve everything that is important to us. That's what this book is about: how you can learn the mindset I've used to train champion athletes and apply it to your life.

At the highest levels, everyone is the best. How can you become better than the best?

If you're a CrossFit Games athlete, it's a question you spend a lot of time considering. Every competitor at the CrossFit Games is physically and mentally formidable. Everyone has areas where they shine a little brighter or struggle a bit more; but on the whole, the differences in physical ability are negligible. So, what are the separators? How do you train to come out on top?

When preparing athletes for the CrossFit Games, I follow a hierarchy of development outlined in the pyramid below. It starts with the development of the *person*, of the character traits necessary to achieve at a high level. These character traits enable my athletes to follow a rigorous *process* designed to utilize every minute of every day toward improvement and progress. The process allows us to maximize every ounce of their *abilities*, which in turn shape our *strategy*.

Most people focus on the top two—ability and strategy. If you're a football team, ability is the strength and conditioning work in the gym and practice and drills out on the field. It's about increasing your speed, agility, and power. It's about running a faster 40 and increasing your bench press. For a football team, strategy is about getting better at the playbook; it's play calling, developing game-by-game battle plans, and executing on the field.

The bottom two parts of the pyramid—person and process—are typically less of a priority. Process is about defining the controllables that can make you a better performer and maximizing your capabilities in every single one of those areas with a commitment bordering on obsession.

Committing to the right process is a critical part of success, but it it's no magic pill. There's no one giant step that will get you from where you are to where you want to be. If you want a six-pack, nothing you can do today will get you a six-pack tomorrow. If you're growing a business, there's no single step that will get you from ten customers today to ten thousand customers tomorrow. It doesn't work that way. The only thing that works is pounding on your craft, day in and day out, doing the right things over and over and over again. As Tim Grover, personal trainer to Michael Jordan and Kobe Bryant, says in his book *Relentless*, "There are no secrets, there are no tricks. If anything, it's the opposite: Whether you are a pro athlete or a guy running a business, or driving a truck or going to school, it's simple. Ask yourself where you are now and where you want to be instead. Ask yourself what you're willing to do to get there. Then make a plan to get there."

Think of it this way: If you were a robot, and things like sleep, relaxation, stress, relationships, desires, and temptations were not a factor, how would you program yourself to meet your goals? How much time would you spend on training? What are the exact quantities and ratios of nutrients that you would consume to fuel yourself? How would you recover? What books, high achievers, and game films would you study? Regardless of your chosen sport or profession, the process is the road map designed to get you from where you are to where you want to be.

Guess what? It's really hard.

We're not robots; we're humans. If it were as simple as just writing it down and putting it on the fridge, everyone would be a champion. Committing to a process requires a unique set of character traits—things like grit, resilience, accountability, confidence, optimism, perseverance, and passion. Without these traits, it's impossible to follow a championship process, which is why character is the first thing I focus on when developing CrossFit Games athletes—the bottom of the pyramid: person.

We're not focusing on character for character's sake. I don't need my athletes to be polite at the dinner table; I want them to win. If I didn't think character was so instrumental to winning, I wouldn't dedicate any time to it. But it is, so I do. In his outstanding book *How Champions Think*, Dr. Bob Rotella, the renowned sports psychologist, has this to say about character: "Whatever the endeavor, I've come to the conclusion that the most successful people have some of what we call natural talent, but not so much that it makes them complacent. They're brimming over with the character traits that promote patient, persistent, hard work. Their physical talents are sufficient to persuade them that they can be as successful as they want to be, but only if they work very hard and work very smart."

That's what this book is about—the blind and relentless pursuit of excellence. It is the story about building the world's fittest athletes, as told through the 2016 CrossFit Games. But this book is not just for elite athletes. It's for anyone who wants to figure out just how good they can possibly become. Whether you're an entrepreneur trying to break through, or you want to be a better doctor, a better mom, or a better middle school basketball coach, this book is about how you can become the champion of what's important to you.

It starts with commitment.

CHAPTER 1

COMMITMENT

★

*Opportunity is missed by most people because
it is dressed in overalls and looks like work.*

—THOMAS EDISON

TUESDAY, JULY 19, 2016

MANHATTAN BEACH MARRIOTT HOTEL

CARSON, CA

In the CrossFit-produced documentary of the 2016 CrossFit Games, commentator Rory McKernan observed that "being a CrossFit Games athlete is basically a mental illness."

By that definition, the Marriott Hotel in Manhattan Beach,

California, where I am currently having dinner, is an insane asylum. The fittest eighty athletes in the world are assembled here, at the host hotel of the CrossFit Games, for the annual welcome reception that kicks off the week-long quest to find the Fittest Man and Woman among them.

I am here because I am coach to three of them—Katrín Davíðsdóttir, Mathew Fraser, and Cole Sager. Like everyone else in this room, they are professional athletes. In the ten years since the first CrossFit Games took place on a small Northern California ranch, the sport of fitness has evolved into a full-time occupation for those who choose to pursue it at the highest level. What started as a friendly get-together in 2007 has morphed into a world-class sporting event, unparalleled in its variance, comprehensiveness, and toughness.

And for good reason—if the goal is legitimately to find the "Fittest on Earth," the test has to be unlike any other. The CrossFit Games test fitness across every physical skill—strength, speed, power, conditioning, endurance, coordination, balance, agility, accuracy, flexibility, and stamina. There is truly no test of fitness anywhere in the world like it. People have compared the Games to the Decathlon, ultra-endurance races, or the Ironman, but those events test a specific facet of human fitness;

the Games test *everything*. From the endurance of ocean swims to skills like handstand walking, from strength required of max-effort Olympic lifts to the stamina of triathlons, from the fortitude of rowing a half marathon to the explosiveness of sprinting over hurdles, from the grace of gymnastics rings to the grit of racing up mountains with sandbags, there is no test in the world that is more comprehensive or more brutal.

Making it to the Games is impossibly difficult. Only the top 0.012 percent of the world's athletes compete under the bright lights every summer to vie for the title of "Fittest on Earth." The qualifying process starts in the winter with the Open, a five-week, five-workout competition held in CrossFit affiliates and garage gyms around the world. In 2016, 302,000 people from 120 different countries participated. The top forty men and top forty women from eight regions then advance to the next stage, Regionals, which take place over a three-day period in May. Only the top five men and top five women from each region advance to the Games, which is held in late July of each year.

Making it to the CrossFit Games takes a commitment that is hard for most people to fathom. The athletes at the highest level of our sport train five to ten hours a day, year-round, to prepare for one week of competition. They commit themselves to a life of discipline, hardship, sacrifice, and suffering. To get to the Games, you have to be world-class at everything and weak in nothing. The sheer workload and physical capabilities of these athletes is literally rewriting exercise physiology books; where it was once considered impossible to run a five-minute mile or deadlift 500 pounds, the *average* male Games competitor can now deadlift over 500 pounds, run just over a five-minute mile, do 50 unbroken pull-ups, and lift 350 pounds over his head. With physical abilities continuing to rise every year, athletes look for competitive edges in every facet of their lives. They weigh, measure, and record their nutrient intake. They have specific sleep protocols. They work weekly with chiropractors, ART specialists, massage therapists, and physical therapists. They have personal muscle stimulation units that they use on a daily basis. They use float tanks to speed up recovery.

Still, nothing is guaranteed. Even if you manage to maximize all those things, you probably still won't make it to the CrossFit Games. Cole Sager, a multiyear Games veteran who finished seventh at the 2015 Games, almost didn't make it back this year. Going into the last workout of Regionals, he was sitting in ninth place, four spots out of contention. Hopping from ninth to fifth in a single event is basically impossible; it's an insurmountable task. It's like coming back from a 27–3 deficit with under three minutes left in the third quarter of the Super Bowl (*Go Pats!*).

It's exactly what Cole did. The final event was a quick, high-power contest with little margin for error, and events like that always have the potential to shake up the leaderboard. In a short sprint of legless rope climbs and barbell thrusters, Cole blazed through, flying up and down the rope in seeming defiance of gravity and went unbroken on the thrusters. He won the event, leapfrogged four competitors, and punched his ticket to the 2016 Games.

After the West Regional podium ceremony, we went out for a celebratory postcompetition dinner. Cole, euphoric from the theatrics of the final event, couldn't stop smiling. "You did it," I told him. "You made it back to the Games. You ready to start working hard?" Cole looked at me like I was crazy. He didn't say it out loud, but I could see the thought on his face—*I just qualified for the Games, man. How have I not been working hard?*

It wasn't that Cole hadn't worked hard, or that we hadn't put a ton of work in together to get him back to the Games; but believing that he was working as hard as he possibly could was a false sense of security. He had yet to learn what the peak of his capacity was. To compete at the limit of his potential at the Games, he needed to shift his mindset to a place where the work was only just beginning.

I told him he'd been doing this sport at an amateur level,

and while he'd been really successful, he was still an amateur. "Are you ready to go pro? If you're not up for it, that's cool. You'll go to the Games, and do well. But if you want to win, I'll give you everything I have. I'll dedicate everything to making it happen. But I'm not going to go all in unless you are. If you're willing to go there with me, knowing how hard this will be, we'll be in it together."

Cole is the kind of person who hears tough feedback and doesn't deflect, doesn't defend, doesn't take it personally; he just listens and then makes his choice. He was quiet as I laid it out for him, listening intently, his head bobbing in acknowledgment. When I was done, he'd already made up his mind. He moved out to Boston for the summer to train with me and Katrín. Over the last few months, I've watched Cole work harder than he's ever worked before. As a result, the Cole sitting a few tables over from me now is at a whole new level as an athlete.

As I watch the three of them from across the room, it occurs to me, not for the first time, how outwardly different they are. Katrín, who is from Iceland, is like a real-life Disney princess. She's the ultimate girly girl—her platinum blonde hair always looks perfect, and she is mortally terrified of insects. Mat is from New England and looks more like a member of Hells Angels—he has a scruffy beard, wiry brown hair, lots of tattoos and he swears a lot. Cole, by contrast, is a clean-cut, all-American type with the physique of a professional running back and the personality of a Golden Retriever. The three of them could not be more different, and yet, they're the same. Beyond their extraordinary physical abilities, they share a set of attitudes and attributes that are paramount to their success—discipline, commitment, passion, confidence, persistence, resiliency, competitiveness, coachability, growth-mindedness, humility, hunger, dedication, tenacity, and grit.

Working and training at the champion level isn't for everybody. It's just not. There's so much pain, so much sacrifice, so many hours, so much sheer monotony and minutiae; there's *so much* you have to think about and dedicate yourself to—to chase perfection. It's not about talent. Everyone at the highest level of any field is talented. It's about commitment. Given this, it's not hard to understand why, for many of the athletes gathered at the Marriott tonight, just being here is the prize. For most people, making it to the top level is enough. They pat themselves on the back, collect their free Reebok swag, and enjoy the competition. They know they don't stand a chance of actually winning, but they can call themselves a *Games athlete*, one of the most venerable distinctions in our sport.

This isn't uncommon, and it isn't unique to the CrossFit

Games. Lots of people put in serious work for a while in pursuit of their goals, and eventually get to a place where they're comfortable. They may not have achieved *all* their long-term goals, but they have achieved a good 90 percent, and they feel that they've checked all the boxes and are doing well enough to be satisfied. They achieve a high level of success in their chosen field; they are, by all accounts, accomplished doctors, teachers, or business owners. That's great. That's laudable. But that's not excellence.

Excellence is maximizing everything you have in the categories that matter to your long-term goals. The categories that matter are different in each craft; for athletes, those categories are training, nutrition, sleep, recovery, and mindset. If you're a brain surgeon or a CEO, your categories may be different. No matter what your craft is, there's a question you should continually ask yourself: *Am I committing everything I have to make myself the tiniest percentage better than I am right now, no matter how hard I have to work, no matter what I have to give up, no matter how long it takes?*

Consider the following graph.

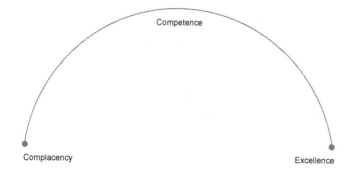

On one end you have complacency, and on the far other end you have excellence. Complacency, at its furthest limit, is a trait that keeps people on the couch. Truly complacent people don't care about excellence, and they don't think it matters. Excellence, on the other hand, we know well; we recognize it in the best and brightest among us, those at the peak of their craft. It's telling yourself that you don't care how hard something is or how long it takes—you're going to give it everything you've got.

The midpoint between complacency and excellence is competence. That, in and of itself, may surprise you; competence is often what people aim for as an endpoint. Most people sit somewhere around that point. They've got some sort of skill set and the semblance of drive; they *want* to be good, but when faced with the work required to be great, they shrug and tell themselves, *Meh, I'm good enough.*

Nobody wants to be at the complacency end, which is

essentially, as far as life is concerned, the bottom. The bottom sucks. The bottom is crappy relationships, scraping by with jobs you hate, unhappiness, addiction. The excellence end is where we all want to be; it's where the ultra-high achievers we all try to emulate are. It's pure aspiration. It's where people like Michael Phelps live.

If you don't think about things too hard, if you never get serious, you'll probably wind up somewhere in the middle, with the vast majority of everyone else. Competence, in and of itself, can be an emotional roller coaster because at a basic level of competence, sometimes you succeed and sometimes you fail, and you're subject to the natural ups and downs of circumstance. If you're a bench player in the NBA, and in one season you get lots of play time—and maybe the game-winning shot—that's a massive success. If you miss that game-winning shot, you've missed what might be your *only* shot. If you're Michael Jordan, however, and you miss a game-winning shot, you're disappointed, but you're not crying yourself to sleep at night. At the excellence end of the curve, you're secure in who you are and you know you're doing everything you can.

A lot of people will consider this spectrum and conclude that they are on the excellence side, simply because they work hard and have achieved a certain level of success in their chosen field. But that's not how it works. Just because you're working hard doesn't mean you're committed, not in the way a champion is, and it doesn't automatically equal excellence. Nowhere is this more apparent than at the CrossFit Games. As CrossFit Games commentator Sean Woodland aptly said, "You don't know how good you have to be just to *suck* at the CrossFit Games." The last-place finisher at the Games may be one of the fittest human beings ever to walk the face of the Earth, but the spectrum is relative; compared to the top-ten finishers, his training, nutrition, recovery, sleep, and mindset are merely competent. At the Games, "world-class" is the just price of admission. To be competitive, you have to be *better* than world-class.

Excellence requires short-term pain for long-term gain. It's painful, in the short term, to get up at 5:00 a.m. and work out; it's painful to say no to a cookie. Long-term, though, the habits add up to incredible gain. Complacency is the exact opposite setup: short-term gain for long-term pain. For instance, if you snooze your alarm, you feel a little better in that moment; you get five more minutes of sleep. If you do it every day, your productivity suffers in the long term. As I tell my athletes, a lot of people are working hard; very, very few people are working really, *really* hard.

People who exist at the excellence end of the bell curve

are focused on long-term gain. People successful in life, in business, and in relationships are living into a process that leads to excellence; these are the people who get up early to work out, who say no to crappy food, who carve out time for learning and mindfulness. They take the time to establish what's important to them and what habits will get them where they want to go. They don't get hung up on the short term. It can't be overstated—that's *hard*. It's a constant dedication to habits and values that can be isolating. In the long term, though, the benefit will be unmatched.

It's easier said than done. I give the same pep talk I gave Cole after Regionals to all my athletes before they get serious with me. I want to make sure they realize that taking the next step, leveling up to champion, will be much harder than they think. I have very simple but specific expectations of my athletes, and they know those expectations up front. They have to be willing to learn, willing to invest the time—as long as it takes—to find the best way. They have to be passionate about wanting to be the best. They have to commit themselves to the process, every single day.

Commitment at this level means being focused on each minute of every day as a space to be perfected. It means devoting yourself to what others see as meaningless detail.

You're focused not on the outcome of your dedication, but on the dedication itself and the person you are trying to become. Those who live in this space aren't just the top 20 percent; they're the true cream of the crop, the top 1 percent of the 1 percent. The three athletes I coach fall into this category. Katrín, Mat, and Cole don't train all year just to make it to the Games and enjoy the ride. They're in it because they want to find out exactly how good they can possibly be. They wake up every morning with one goal in mind—becoming better. They're here to *win*.

As if reading my mind, CrossFit Games director Dave Castro strides into the room. After a few pleasantries, he tells the athletes, "This year will be the most physically and mentally challenging CrossFit Games ever. The ten-year anniversary is going to push you to limits you didn't know you had," he says, both a threat and a promise. "There are going to be times when you'll be scared," he continues in typical Dave fashion. "You're not going to want to be doing some of the stuff we're doing. You're going to question what we're doing. You're going to question why you're here." Dave, a former Navy SEAL instructor, loves playing these psychological games. With a taunting smile he adds, "If at any point you are scared or are questioning those motives, please feel free to come up to me or any of our staff, and we'll gladly pull you out and make you comfortable and you'll be done with the competition." After a slight pause for dramatics he concludes, "This is about trying to win the CrossFit Games. If you're not coming for that reason, you should just quit now."

Then he turns and walks out.

Let the Games begin.

CHAPTER 2

GRIT

Today I will do what others won't so
tomorrow I can do what others can't.

—JERRY RICE

WEDNESDAY, JULY 20, 2016

AROMAS, CA

Tuesday night is an athlete briefing at the Marriott. In years past, this is where one or two of the first events of the Games are announced. Instead, Dave takes to the podium to say only that the athletes will meet at 3:30 tomorrow morning in the lobby. "If you are not there at that time, the bus is leaving without you and your CrossFit Games are over," he says gravely, then dismisses the competitors to go get some sleep.

The only clues to tomorrow's adventure come in the form of a cryptic packing list—valid photo ID, gloves, lifting belt, tactical pants, towel, hat, sunglasses, three pairs of shorts, sweatshirt. The athletes pore over the lists as though they contain invisible treasure maps. *Where are we going? Why do we have to bring this stuff? When are we coming back?* Scott Panchik, a Games veteran, cracks that this is like the Hunger Games.

The next morning, I wake up at 3:00 a.m. and meet up with Matt O'Keefe. Officially, O'Keefe is Katrín, Mat, and Cole's agent. He travels with them whenever they're on the road to help with the endless details and arrangements of being a pro athlete—from handling sponsor and media requests, to renting cars and hotel rooms, to scheduling bodywork. But "agent" barely scratches the surface of O'Keefe's importance to our team. He knows Katrín and Mat as well as I do—they affectionately refer to him as "Dad"—and his presence here is as integral to their performance as nutrition and recovery.

O'Keefe and I go collect Katrín, who is not known for her punctuality, from her room, then head downstairs to find Mat and Cole. What was once a dignified hotel lobby is, by 3:20 a.m., a hoard of sleepy athletes, judges, and event staff. Bags and brightly colored gear are strewn everywhere—the Marriott looks like the staging ground for a festive land and sea invasion. At 3:30, the athletes are corralled into an adjacent ballroom for a briefing, where Dave informs them they're headed to LAX. He tells them to make their bags flight-ready, then walks out.

The room immediately erupts. *A flight! Where are we going?* For the next half hour, rumors fly around the lobby at a furious pace as high-strung athletes work themselves into a state about possible destinations. Mat, meanwhile, could not possibly be more relaxed. O'Keefe and I find him in the lobby—eating a banana and thumbing through his phone—and you can practically see the anxiety of the room flowing around him, like lava around a rock. When one of the other athletes asks him to guess where they're heading, he just shrugs. "Wherever we're going, we're all going there together," he says, impassively.

Around 4:00 a.m., as the competitors begin boarding the waiting charter buses outside, Justin Bergh, general manager of the CrossFit Games, briefs the coaches. Where they're going, you'll not be allowed to follow, he tells us. We won't have contact with our athletes in person until they return from this off-site event.

It's going to be a long day.

* * *

I get a text from Mat around 6:00 a.m. He's just received his boarding pass, which lists their destination as San Jose. That can only mean one thing. They're going to the Ranch.

The Ranch is CrossFit legend. Back in 2007, before Cross-Fit was a household name, before the StubHub Center, title sponsors, and prime-time ESPN coverage, a group of seventy friends got together on Dave Castro's family's ranch in Aromas, California, to see who among them was the most fit. The inaugural CrossFit Games consisted of three workouts over the course of two days and attracted about 150 spectators. It was the unknown and the unknow-able brought to life. Then, as now, details of the events were not released until the start of competition.

Aromas is like the Mesopotamia of the CrossFit world. Taking the competition back there this year, for the tenth anniversary of the Games, is a masterstroke. The sur-prise trip will allow a new generation of Games athletes to experience the iconic mecca that gave birth to our sport, and will test their fitness outside the familiar confines of StubHub's soccer and tennis stadiums. With no coaches, no crowd, and no pump-up music, it will also be a terrific mental test.

O'Keefe and I get breakfast in the now-quiet Marriott, and then, for lack of anything else to do, go work out. We arrive in the hotel ballroom, which has been transformed into a full-scale CrossFit gym for the week, and discover we're not the only ones with this idea. Many of the other coaches are also milling around, unsure of what to do, like parents on the first day of school. The atmosphere in here is comically similar to the lobby earlier this morning—now that the Ranch has been confirmed as the destination, speculation has moved on to the next set of uncontrollables. *What will the events be? How many workouts will the athletes do today? Will they retest events from the 2007 Games or the 2008 Games?* It's a guessing game none of us can win, so O'Keefe and I do five rounds of front squats, GHD sit-ups, rowing, and kettlebell swings instead.

We find out the day's events the same way everyone else does—by refreshing the CrossFit Games website every ten minutes until the workouts are released to the public. The first two workouts are a repeat of the first two events from the 2009 Games: a 7K trail run, followed by a deadlift ladder. Naturally, the run course will be more difficult than in 2009, and the deadlift ladder is much heavier. The third workout is a beefed-up version of the 2009 sandbag run, an event widely regarded as one the most brutal in Games history. This time, however, the athletes will do 50 wallball shots and 25 weighted GHD sit-ups prior to sprinting up the infamous hill with their medicine ball.

EVENT 1:	EVENT 2:	EVENT 3:
Trail Run	Deadlift Ladder	Ranch Mini Chipper
For Time:		For Time:
7K Trail Run		50 Wallball Shots (30/20 lb.)
		24 Medball
		GHD Sit-Ups
		Hill Sprint with Medball

A shaky, handheld Facebook Live feed ends up being the only coverage of the first event. We wait for the trail run to start, and the ballroom/gym starts to feel like a waiting room at the doctor's office. The other coaches are speculating about who will win. On the women's side, everyone's money is on Samantha Briggs. *Safe bet.* On the men's side, Josh Bridges, a former Navy SEAL, is the favorite. Brent Fikowski is a close second. O'Keefe and I exchange looks. *We'll see about that.*

The trail run starts innocently enough, on a wide, straight road. The men and women are running together, and the first few minutes are a stampede as the athletes jockey for position. I watch the Facebook Live feed and observe the wide range of clothing choices. Some athletes, like Mat, are in their usual gym attire—shorts and no shirt. Others, anticipating what they might encounter on the trail, have opted to wear the tactical pants that were issued for this event. Some are even wearing gloves. As they hit the woods, you can see the appeal—the trail is narrow, steep, and covered in rocks and brush.

Five minutes in, Mat is out in front, and it's obvious that everyone else is competing for second place. He wins the event, a full minute and a half in front of second-place finisher Josh Bridges. He jogs casually across the finish line and flashes the camera a thumbs-up. He doesn't even look tired. The comments in the Facebook Live feed oscillate between shock and awe. It doesn't make sense—Mat is known as a weightlifter. He's not supposed to win running events.

Everyone is surprised, but they shouldn't be. This is classic Mat. It's how he got here in the first place.

People remember Mat bursting onto the CrossFit scene when he won the 2014 East Regional. Almost everyone refers to 2014 as his rookie season, but it wasn't. He was there in 2013, too. The reason no one remembers it is because it wasn't particularly memorable. At the North East Regional that year, Mat, a former Junior National Weightlifting Champion, did well in events involving moving a barbell, but had obvious holes in his game. He finished fifth overall, two spots out of contention for the

Games. Instead of being demoralized, he was heartened—it was his first time interacting with Games-caliber athletes up close, and he walked away thinking, *If I work hard and practice, I could beat them.*

In his first appearance at the CrossFit Games, in 2014, Mat took second overall. The following year, in 2015, he placed second again. He is referred to as a prodigy, a natural. For obvious reasons, people focus on his physical abilities—Mat is, without question, an extraordinarily talented athlete. But it's his other, less visible qualities that make him the champion he is.

The main one is grit.

What is grit, really? It's a word that's been used to describe everything under the sun, but it means something specific: when things get hard, you push harder; when you fail, you get back up stronger; when you don't see results, you don't get discouraged, but you just continue to pound away day, after day, after day, with relentlessness, consistency, heart, and passion—that's grit.

Mat consciously, every day, seeks out things he might be bad at. When he finds weaknesses, he doesn't just work on them—he *eviscerates* them. One of the events he struggled with at the 2013 North East Regional was "Jackie," a

CrossFit benchmark workout of rowing, barbell thrusters, and pull-ups. He got dusted on the row—the other men were pulling 1:40 splits, and he was struggling to hold on to 1:50. That put him twenty seconds slower than the leaders, which was an enormous, unsurmountable gap. Relative to his competitors, he straight-up sucked at rowing. After Regionals, he went home, bought a rower, and for the next year, he rowed 4,000 to 5,000 meters of intervals—*every day*.

Even at the elite level, punishing yourself with thirty minutes of high-intensity rowing intervals every day isn't the norm, but for Mat it wasn't even a question. He's the kind of competitor who sees a gap between where he is and where he needs to be, and takes immediate and unrelenting steps to close it. It's not a question of how much work it will take, how much suffering will be involved, or how fast the results will come. It's about committing to the grind every day.

Last year, at the 2015 CrossFit Games, Mat got wrecked by an odd-object event involving the Pig, a 580-pound, refrigerator-like object that the competitors had to flip down the soccer field. When he got home from the Games, he bought one. For the next six months, he went into the gym every Sunday, late at night when it was empty, and flipped it for *hours*. Thirty flips, then sixty flips for time.

One hundred flips for time. He made sure that if it ever came up again, he'd be as prepared as he could be. It's the same way Mat approaches everything in his life. When he was in school, he would sit in the library for ten hours on a Saturday and read textbooks cover to cover. When he finished a chapter, if he couldn't recite every single law or formula by heart, he would go back and read it again.

No one loves doing rowing intervals, max-effort squats, or studying for ten hours at a time. As Mat would say, *That shit hurts.* There's nothing fun about waking up and doing things you're bad at, over and over again. It takes an extraordinary amount of grit to commit yourself to that brand of torture. Given this, it's no surprise that the average person doesn't aspire to grit; they aspire to talent. Imagine two players on a college basketball team. One has a 43-inch vertical leap, can nail three-pointers all day, and barely practices. People say, *He's a natural; he was born to do this.* The other player is the first one into practice every single day. He wins every team sprint. He's the best defensive player on the team; he fights for rebounds and dives for loose balls with no regard for himself. He's the consummate teammate: dedicated, resilient, committed, all in.

If you asked one hundred college students which player they'd rather be, ninety-nine of them would say they'd rather be the one with the God-given talent. In our society, we reward talent above all else, even though talent isn't what wins in the long run. To win, you have to be talented, yes. But talent without grit is just potential. Talent plus grit is unstoppable.

People see talent, like Mat's, but they fail to see the hard work behind it. The idea of "God-given talent" gives the rest of us an out, if you think about it. *You* weren't blessed with incredible once-in-a-generation skills, so you get a pass for not achieving once-in-a-generation success. What people don't see is that behind most every talented person who has become a massive success is a daily schedule of grind, hours of suck, and a whole string of difficult, lonely moments working on the tiny details that will get them where they want to go.

Author Daniel Coyle wrote a book called *The Talent Code*, in which he investigates the true nature of talent and how it corresponds to success. In the book, he studies people generally regarded by society as phenomenally talented, and breaks down how much work and practice is actually involved in their achievements. For instance, take Mozart. Widely regarded as one of the greatest musical geniuses of all time, Mozart had true God-given talent. Or did he? What people either forget or don't know is that Mozart was also a slave to his craft. By the time he was twenty-eight years old, his hands had become deformed because of the thousands of hours he spent playing and composing. That's the missing element in the popular portrait of Mozart. Yes, he had a gift that set him apart from others. Yes, he was born into a family of composers. Yes, he was the most complete musician imaginable, one who wrote for all instruments in all combinations. Still, few people, even those hugely gifted, are capable of the grit that Mozart displayed throughout his life. As Mozart himself wrote to a friend, "People err who think my art comes easily to me. I assure you, dear friend, nobody has devoted so much time and thought to composition as I. There is not a famous master whose music I have not industriously studied through many times."

People want to boil down elite achievement to "born with it" talent; it gives them an excuse for why they're not at the same level. They don't want to hear about the hours upon hours upon hours of patient, meticulous practice that achiever went through to get where they are. The grit with which Mat is willing to pursue excellence in his craft is the reason that a former weightlifter with no cardiovascular endurance just won a 7K trail run against the fittest men in the world.

And it's why he's in first place at the end of the first day of competition.

After three grueling events in Aromas, the athletes load back onto the buses and return to the airport to catch a late flight back to Los Angeles. It's been a long day; by the time they return, they'll have been traveling and competing for eighteen hours. For most of the competitors, this is not ideal, particularly since the next event is an early morning swim at the beach tomorrow. For this reason, it's great for my athletes. The tougher things get, the more we thrive. The more uncomfortable the other competitors are, the greater our advantage. As if to illustrate this point, Mat texts me from the airport: "Flight delayed, won't be back until midnight."

As I'm reading it, the typing bubbles appear again: "Good."

I smile. This Mat is dangerous.

CHAPTER 3

POSITIVITY

★

*It's not what you look at that
matters, it's what you see.*

—HENRY DAVID THOREAU

THURSDAY, JULY 21, 2016
REDONDO BEACH, CA

Back in Los Angeles, Day 2 of competition dawns clear
and cool. Thursday is historically a rest day during the
CrossFit Games, but not this year—the athletes will take
to the beach first thing this morning.

EVENT 4:
Ocean Swim

For Time:
500 m Swim

As Katrín, O'Keefe, and I make our way to breakfast, the lobby is buzzing about the rigors of yesterday's competition and travel schedule. The return flight from the Aromas adventure was delayed by three hours last night, preventing any of the athletes from getting to bed until well after midnight. This morning they were up again before 5:30 to prep for the early swim event. Three events, two flights, hours of delays, no sleep, compete again. I'm psyched. The Games could not be off to a better start.

Not all of the competitors share my enthusiasm. Several are openly discussing the merits of boycotting today's swim. *If none of us show up, they can't make us do it*, one of the women competitors says, and I can't tell if she's joking or not.

Down on the beach, the complaining continues. Games documentarian Sevan Matossian asks one of the women, a three-year Games veteran, how she's feeling after yesterday's slugfest at the Ranch. Her response was included in the CrossFit-produced behind-the-scenes 2016 Games documentary:

Waiting in the airport for so long at night, then having to get up really early, was really tiring. It's already a lot harder than it was two years ago. The first day—everything from getting up early to three workouts in one day—that was a lot harder than what we did in 2014, when all we did on the first day was an ocean swim and then an overhead squat. I felt a lot better going into Thursday. And now we're swimming on Thursday, so we don't even get a rest day.

A few minutes later, Sevan finds Katrín, who is emerging from a warm-up dip in the surf. He asks her the same question. Here's what she says:

I feel good! I was able to sleep a lot yesterday. I slept on the airport floor, I slept the whole plane ride, then I slept for five hours when I got into bed. I feel really good. I'm happy about that. Love that we get to go straight through with no rest day, love that. The more volume, the better. That's great. So far it's been amazing.

Listening to both interviews, you could be forgiven for thinking that the two women are describing two different competitions. But they're not. They both had the exact same day yesterday. They did the same workouts, they had the same travel issues, and they got the same amount of sleep. The only difference is how they've chosen to perceive it; where one woman sees adversity and difficulty, Katrín sees advantage and opportunity.

Katrín makes sleeping on the airport floor sound like a day at the spa. Her optimism is so convincing that you almost forget that lying on the ground in a noisy public place is uncomfortable and not terribly conducive to sleep or recovery. If you're a professional athlete trying to defend your championship title, it's definitely not ideal. The same can be said for the hour of sleep she got on the plane; everyone who has ever tried to sleep on an airplane knows how restorative that is. Katrín, however, chooses to see the bright side. In her mind, some sleep is better than no sleep.

Staying positive is difficult for humans because our DNA is hardwired to hold on to negative experiences over positive ones, for sheer survival. Way back when our species was in survival mode, it was far more important to know and remember that the big furry animal with claws and teeth would kill you than it was to know and remember that the butterfly was pretty. It was more important to remember which berries would kill you than which ones were tastiest. We developed a survival instinct that is ingrained in a negative mindset.

Negativity, though, is immensely detrimental to performance. When you're in a negative mindset, you're slower and less precise. Positivity, by contrast, is directly linked to improved performance. It doesn't matter what the task or profession is; you could be an athlete, a surgeon, a professional typist, or a classical violinist. If you stay positive, you perform with greater speed and accuracy. You are *better*, across the board. Because of this, I need my athletes in a positive mindset in order to get the work out of them that will maximize their potential. At my gym, there's an unbreakable threefold policy:

NEVER WHINE. NEVER COMPLAIN.
NEVER MAKE EXCUSES.

This is easier said than done. Not only is negativity hard-wired into our DNA; it's become ingrained in our culture: almost two-thirds of English words convey the negative side of things. Positivity, therefore, must be a learned behavior. Some people are privileged to be raised with an optimistic worldview; but for just as many, it's an attitude they consciously choose to have. Katrín is a very positive person, but that doesn't mean she didn't have to work at it, and that she doesn't continue to work at it every day. What comes across as effortless optimism in her interview on the beach is something we've consciously worked on for years.

For example, this past winter, I had Katrín do a long warm-up outside. It was February in Boston, and it was *cold*. When she came back into the gym afterward, steam was flowing off her shoulders, and she was blowing hard on her hands to get some heat back into them. I asked her how the warm-up went for her. She gave me her times for each section, and told me her thoughts on the difficulty of the warm-up and her overall approach. Then she said, "And it was...uh, never mind."

She'd been about to say, "It was really cold," but she's conditioned not to complain to the point where something like that—which to others, is simply stating a fact about the weather—physically can't make its way out of her mouth. Saying that it's cold outside may appear to be simply stating a fact, but it's actually more detrimental than it might seem in the short term. Focusing on negative feelings or circumstances—*It's so hot out. I'm tired. This traffic sucks. My boss is such an idiot*—brings greater focus to things that are ultimately outside of your control and are potentially detrimental to your performance. In no competitive or life scenario will focusing on negative uncontrollable factors improve your performance or stress levels.

An optimistic mindset is a distinguishable characteristic of elite performers because what the human mind focuses on and talks about is what we see more of. Stanford professor

Arnold Zwicky calls this the "frequency illusion," which is essentially a phenomenon that causes you to see more of the things you're already focused on. This is caused, he says, by two psychological processes.

The first process, selective attention, kicks in when you're struck by a new word, thing, or idea; after that, you unconsciously keep an eye out for it, and as a result you find it surprisingly more often. The second process, confirmation bias, reassures you that each sighting is further proof of your impression that the thing has gained overnight omnipresence. Think about the last time you bought a new car. Let's say it was a Jeep Grand Cherokee. After you buy it, you start noticing them *everywhere*—it seems that every third person on the road is driving a Jeep Grand Cherokee. And you don't just notice colors— you notice the different models and add-ons; Laredos are more common than Limiteds, and there are fewer SRTs than there are Overlands. Obviously, there was not a sudden surge in local Jeep sales the day you bought your car. But because you're actively thinking about it, you can't help but notice them everywhere. The same principle applies to your mindset toward sports, work, and relationships. If you talk about (or worse, complain about) things that are outside of your control, things that could diminish performance, you will see and experience more of those things.

Down on Redondo Beach, Katrín is doing something we've talked about and practiced hundreds of times: she's telling herself the right story. We all have stories we tell ourselves, and whether we realize it or not, they dictate what we are capable of. As Ryan Holiday writes in *The Obstacle Is the Way*, "There is no good or bad without us, there is only perception. There is the event itself and the story we tell ourselves about what it means." If your story is telling you you're not good enough, not smart enough, too old, too young, or can't do it, your subconscious will believe you.

Diet is an area where this commonly shows up. People tell themselves all manner of negative stories regarding their inability to lose weight. They'll clean up their diet and hit the gym hard for a few weeks, and then get discouraged when progress is slow. "I'm just big-boned," they say, or they'll chalk it up to genetics and a slow metabolism before going back to eating crap and skipping workouts. We're all guilty of this in one way or another. For me, it's technology. I've never been tech savvy—I'm the guy who won't upgrade his phone until the iPhone 3 that I've been using for half a decade is discontinued. I am forty years old, but when it comes to technology I might as well be 105. If it's more complicated than changing the batteries, I ask my wife for help. If I have to so much as change a font in a PowerPoint presentation, I call my gym's media director. I tell myself that I am not good at understanding technology, so it's become a self-fulfilling prophecy—because I hate technology, I studiously avoid it, which ensures that I remain incompetent at using it, which makes me hate it all the more.

The flip side of this is equally powerful. If you tell yourself, as Katrín does, that no amount of adversity can throw you off your game, you're far more likely to be resilient and thus successful in the long run. Your thoughts become your words, your words become your actions, and your actions dictate your destiny. Down on the beach, the swim hasn't even started yet, but Katrín's mindset has already given her a competitive advantage—in her mind, she's fresh and rested, while half the field is telling themselves they're sleep-deprived and off their game.

O'Keefe and I watch from a nearby lifeguard tower as the athletes make their way to the starting line. When Dave blasts the foghorn, eighty bodies leap forward as one. They're at full tilt after just a few seconds, and it's a stampede through the sand, followed by a street fight into the water. The men and women are competing together in one heat, which greatly adds to the overall sense of anarchy. It's impossible to tell the athletes apart—they're all wearing the same Games-issued bathing suits and swim caps—so all we can do is stand and wait for Kat, Mat, and Cole to emerge from the surf.

Katrín, who has worked hard to become an above-average swimmer, finally pops out about eight minutes later. She sprints to the finish on shaky legs and takes eleventh, a strong placement. I watch from the sidelines as Cole comes over and hauls her to her feet. She's out of breath for about a minute, and then the two of them are laughing and gesticulating animatedly. Obviously, Katrín owes her performance to a lot more than her glass-half-full mindset. She trains in the pool year-round, and we spent the last month on Cape Cod getting comfortable open-water swimming in the ocean. At the end of the day, it was her preparation, not her attitude, that dictated her results. Positivity doesn't guarantee anything, but it can lower perceived exertion, make things seem more enjoyable, improve your chances of competing at your potential, and give you a competitive advantage.

CHAPTER 4

EMBRACE ADVERSITY

★

*Sometimes when you're in a dark place
you think you've been buried, but
you've actually been planted.*

—UNKNOWN

FRIDAY, JULY 23, 2016

STUBHUB CENTER, CARSON, CA

During Games week, Mat's day starts when O'Keefe knocks on his hotel room door in the morning. It's part of an unspoken ritual that is built into our team—I handle

Katrín, and O'Keefe handles Mat. On Friday, Day 3 of competition, O'Keefe has barely removed his hand from Mat's door when it swings wide open. It's 6:00 in the morning, but Mat greets him like it's noon. The athletes have been competing for two days, but today is the first day of events at the StubHub Center, so it feels like the start of something. Mat is ready.

It will be a full day of competition, but the only event we know about so far is "Murph," taking place first thing this morning.

EVENT 5:
Murph

For Time:
1-Mile Run

Then, 5 Rounds of:
20 Pull-Ups
40 Push-Ups
60 Squats
1-Mile Run

Each athlete will wear weighted body armor (men 20 lb., women 14 lb.) for the duration of the event.

"Murph" is one of the most famous workouts in CrossFit. It's named after Lt. Michael Murphy, a Navy SEAL who was killed in Afghanistan while trying to save the lives of his team. Lt. Murphy had a favorite workout that he did regularly while on base, and it involved exactly the level of physical punishment you'd expect Navy SEALs to find fun. Structurally, it was simple: they'd each put on all their body armor—around 20 pounds of extra weight—and then run a mile. Coming in from the mile, they'd do 100 pull-ups, 200 push-ups, and 300 squats. Then they'd run another mile.

Last year, 2015, his workout was included as a surprise event at the 2015 CrossFit Games for the first time. In CrossFit affiliates around the country, "Murph" is a hallowed Memorial Day tradition. So, when this workout showed up at the Games last year, no one worried too much. Though a long, brutal workout, it's one that seasoned CrossFit athletes have done half a dozen times. The familiarity bred a sense of competency. *At least we know what this feels like*, the athletes thought. *At least we've done this before.*

It turned out that no one had ever done anything like that 2015 Murph. CrossFit Games athletes are renowned for their ability to suffer, but this event tested everyone's limits of endurance, stamina, fortitude, and pain tolerance.

The event started at high noon, in July, in Southern California. Temperature readings on the field were 125 degrees, and the athletes were pouring sweat just waiting for the event to start.

The extreme heat wreaked havoc on the athletes' minds and bodies. Kara Webb, an Australian Games veteran, ran the last mile unconscious, completely blacked out. After she stumbled across the finish line, her head lolling to one side, her limp body was carted off on a stretcher by medics. Two-time Games champion Annie Thorisdottir didn't finish the event at all—she limped out of the stadium for the second mile, almost collapsed at the halfway point, and returned in a slow, disoriented walk. Before reaching the finish line, she was stopped by medics, who diagnosed her with extreme heat exhaustion. She never recovered and, along with a handful of other athletes, withdrew from competition the following day.

With the nightmare of last year's Murph still looming in the athletes' minds, the mood in the warm-up area is somber and timid. The competitors strap on their vests like they're going into battle. While Mat warms up on a treadmill, I spot Brent Fikowski moving through some squats.

Brent, out of Kelowna, British Columbia, is here as a

rookie. The previous two years, at the West Regional, he'd come in just shy of qualifying for the Games. Then, seemingly out of nowhere, he won this year's Regional by a staggering seventy-point margin. I was there, coaching Cole, so after the competition I asked him what the difference had been from missing the Games two years in a row to dominating the field.

He shrugged. "This year I got injured."

He told me that he'd torn his labrum in his hip, and so he had to put aside pretty much all impact training such as running, jumping, and other high-work-capacity activity. Brent is a workhorse with a sick engine; he'd always had incredible work capacity. Where he'd been weak was in his upper-body strength. So, when he tore his hip labrum, he regarded the setback as an opportunity to dedicate all his time to his biggest weakness. He worked tirelessly on his upper-body strength while his hip healed. When it came time for Regionals, he'd gone from a fairly above-average, but always just-off-the-podium athlete to completely dominating the field and blowing the competition out of the water. The adversity he'd faced, an obstacle that might have made another athlete give up their dreams, is literally the reason he's here right now, warming up for Murph.

Psychologists call this adversarial growth. "What doesn't

kill you makes you stronger" is not a cliché but a fact. It's a classic example of the way successful people use adversity to grow and thrive. There is perhaps no better sample size of successful people than the eighty fittest men and women at the CrossFit Games. Elite athletes know something that most people don't—adversity is the best thing that can happen to you. The competitors here at the Games know that humans *only* improve through adversity by embracing short-term pain. Ensuring there is no struggle, no challenge, and staying in your wheelhouse is a recipe for spinning your wheels without improving. It's the days when you have to do things that scare you, when you have to take risks, when you have to push against challenge and difficulty—those are the days that make you stronger, faster, and better overall.

In strength and conditioning circles, this is known as the Overload Principle. It basically states that you can force adaptation in your body by consistently pushing past yesterday's limit; you can make yourself stronger by showing your body what stronger feels like. But in doing this, you're going to experience adversity; you're going to have days that are incredibly challenging, even scary. There are going to be days that cause you to question your motives and ability. It's important to realize that the toughest days are your best days, because they have the potential to force the *most* adaptation—mentally, as well as physically.

Two years ago, I took a small handful of the athletes I was coaching on my dad's boat to Thompson Island, off Boston Harbor, to do some swim training in preparation for the 2015 Games. It was a typical spring day in New England, cold and windy. The ice and snow had melted only weeks ago, so the water was cold, colder than the Pacific where the athletes would be competing a month later. Their task was to jump into the water, swim about 300 meters to shore, wait for everyone to arrive, then swim back to the boat. This training session wasn't designed to hone the skills and technique of open-water swimming, nor the stamina required to compete a relatively short 600-meter swim. That day, I was assessing how they would respond to the fear of the unknown—the cold, and the shortness of breath that happens when your body is shocked by ice water.

The strongest swimmers jumped in with minimal hesitation, but Katrín balked on the back of the boat, like a skittish racehorse reluctantly approaching a starting gate. She stood on the swim platform staring down at the cold water, shivering in her bathing suit, contemplating her options. I heard her mumble to herself, "I can't do this. I'm not getting in." Her eyes began to well up, and a tear rolled down her cheek. After a few minutes of this, I verbally pushed her in the water, and all the athletes began making their way to shore.

They were almost back to the boat when, seemingly out of nowhere, jellyfish started appearing—and not just one or two. There were dinner-plate-sized jellyfish *everywhere*. They were impossible to avoid; the water looked like a bowl of semi-transparent cheerios. With nothing to do but continue swimming, the athletes paddled through them, cutting through a forest of jellyfish tentacles along the way.

Back in the boat, the group was shivering and cold, but buoyant with pride. As they hurriedly wrapped themselves in towels and jumped back into their sweats and hoodies, they high-fived, hugged, and congratulated each other on their accomplishment. *We did it!* was written all over their faces. I congratulated them—and then told them to do it again. For a few seconds, everyone looked at me like I was crazy, or kidding. Then Katrín, to my surprise and delight, threw the towel off her shoulders, turned, and jumped in the water.

It was a small moment, but it was a huge mental milestone for her; she'd transformed from an athlete who contemplated, sat in her own suffering, and played mind games with herself to an athlete who decided that facing her fears with a "just start" mindset was a more productive approach. It was the Overload Principle at its most poignant—in a span of twenty minutes, her standards for what she felt that she could overcome were drastically transformed. When we went to the Games that year and faced the chilly swells of the Pacific, she was confident and calm—she had been through so much worse.

CrossFit Games athletes are not like most people. Most people are afraid of overload. They're afraid of facing adversity, afraid of being uncomfortable. People want to do things they're good at, because it makes them feel and look successful and provides a boost to the ego. It signals to those around them that they're special, talented, gifted.

The problem with limiting yourself to training, practicing, and living within your comfort zone is that it prevents you from growing and reaching your full potential. We need to struggle because the struggle is what makes us better—the struggle is itself the journey. Humans naturally fear adversity, which is ironic because adversity is the only thing that makes us better. We have an instinctive fear of the one thing that is certain to lead to the results we crave. When we know this, the challenges, hardships, and struggles that might seemingly look like setbacks and things to avoid become anything but—they become defining moments that create the most dramatic changes and should be cherished and sought after, not feared and endured.

We fear adversity and do everything we can to avoid it,

even though it is a guaranteed part of life for every species on planet Earth. It's not a matter of if we will encounter it, but only a matter of when. And when we do face it, the form the adversity takes is far less important than how we respond to it.

Getting fired is probably one of the most traumatic examples of professional adversity. There's a social stigma around losing your job—it's embarrassing and perceived as a sign of weakness or failure. We internalize it as an incredible obstacle that we need to suffer through, when, in reality, it's anything but. If you were fired from your job, there's a good chance that you weren't in love with it to begin with. If you were underperforming, it was most likely related to a lack of passion for the daily roles and responsibilities you were tasked with—and if you lacked passion, you probably weren't meant to be doing that job in the first place. Being fired can be terrifying, but it can also force you out of your comfort zone—much like Brent Fikowski getting injured—and provide the opportunity to become a better version of yourself.

There are countless examples of successful people who were fired at some point in their careers before going on to be wildly successful—Steve Jobs was famously fired from Apple before returning to reshape the entire tech industry; Walt Disney was fired from the *Kansas City*

Star because he "lacked imagination and had no good ideas"; J. K. Rowling was fired from her job as a secretary before going on to become the world's first and only billionaire author. Had they not faced these career setbacks, Jobs, Disney, and Rowling might never have become the industry legends we know today. Similarly, Katrín has admitted to me a number of times that she wouldn't be the champion she is today if she hadn't failed to qualify for the Games in 2014. Much like these other titans, Katrín didn't become a champion in spite of her adversity, but *because* of it.

Part of leveraging adversity is expecting it. Coaching and preparing athletes to excel at the CrossFit Games is a uniquely challenging task. Like coaches in other sports, I am responsible for getting my athletes into peak mental and physical shape, game-planning, strategizing, and accounting for every last detail and variable. This is made exponentially more difficult by the fact that we don't know what the tests are going to be until it's too late to prepare for them. In fact, there is only one thing I am absolutely certain is going to happen when we compete at the CrossFit Games, and that is that at some point, things are not going to go according to plan. Last year, we had no way of knowing that it would be 125 degrees during Murph. We trained for the heat (we did sauna sessions during the winter months, sweat tests at varying temperatures, and repeatedly trained at temperatures and humidity that exceeded the expected highs of game day), but no one could have anticipated or trained for that kind of heat. Invariably, things come up that we can't control. We have to accept that competing in our sport, and in life in general, is not completely predictable—and we don't want it to be. In challenges and hardship, the struggle of adapting on the fly is paramount, and the ability to do so is characteristic of all champions. As Darwin said, "It is not the strongest of the species that survives, nor the most intelligent that survives. It is the one that is most adaptable to change."

Visualization is a sports psychology practice that prescribes a mental rehearsal of the outcome you want. The central tenant of visualization is seeing the event the way you want it to unfold. If you're a tennis player, this means imagining hitting your spots on every serve, scorching every backhand down the line, putting away volleys with devastating angles, and cruising to an easy victory.

For years, I practiced visualization in this fashion. I had my athletes visualize perfection, executing flawlessly, achieving their desired outcomes, decimating the competition, and doing it all effortlessly. In 2011, I coached in my gym, CrossFit New England, to win the team competition at the Games and be named Fittest Gym on Earth. That year, I used a detailed visualization before the first event in an attempt to maximize my team's preparation and performance. I took my team into an empty ballroom in the hotel where we were staying and had them lie down and close their eyes.

For ten minutes, I painted a mental picture of perfection. I had them visualize walking onto the field of play, imagining the smell of the grass, the feel of the sun on their faces, and the noise of the announcers and the crowd. I walked them through every repetition, every minute of the performance, emphasizing the precision, grace, and excellence of their execution. I described how they would be in the "zone," and every task would be accomplished seamlessly. I gave them confidence that they would be able to operate and communicate effectively as a team, and that we would win that first event.

However, when we actually went out onto the competition floor, few things went the way I had described. It wasn't from poor mental or physical preparation, or lack of concentration during our visualization exercise—it was because there were certain adversities we hadn't prepared for.

In retrospect, this was hardly surprising. If you visualize everything going perfectly, you can't possibly be prepared when unexpected challenges arise, like equipment malfunctions, breakdowns in communication, errors by teammates or judges, 125-degree heat, or competitors leapfrogging you on the leaderboard. By not preparing for adversity, you're setting yourself up to fail when it arrives. And it will arrive at some point—if life teaches us anything, it's that very few things ever line up exactly the way we want. Visualization is a powerful tool, but it's not enough to simply visualize success. You need to also envision adversity and setbacks. Of course you know how to succeed when things go perfectly. I know the mindset of every athlete when they are getting all the calls, winning, and everything seems to be lining up for them. What I really want to find out is how they will think, act, and perform when things go terribly wrong.

Michael Phelps competes with a championship mindset and exemplifies what it means to visualize and expect adversity. During the 200-meter Butterfly at the Beijing Olympic Games, Phelps was contending for his tenth Olympic gold medal, which would have made him the most decorated Olympian of all time. He already held the world record for the event and, as he stepped onto the starting platform, he was favored to win by a comfortable margin.

Then disaster struck—as soon as Phelps dove in, his

goggles started filling with water. By the time he reached the turnaround, he couldn't see anything at all. Despite this, he never missed a beat; if you watch the video, you can't even tell there is a problem. He wins a gold medal and breaks his own world record while swimming *completely blind*. At the most elite level of competition, Michael Phelps overcame an obstacle that would have ruined the chances of almost everyone else. How did he do it?

By expecting adversity—and expecting to overcome it.

In training, Phelps engages in a different kind of visualization. He envisions the entire race, stroke by stroke, from start to finish. But he doesn't just rehearse the perfect race. He visualizes everything that could possibly go wrong, then visualizes how he'll respond. So when his goggles filled with water in the 200-meter final, he didn't need to panic—he already knew exactly how to handle it.

Expecting adversity is a hallmark of many successful people, and it extends well beyond the world of sports. Imagine that you are giving a sales presentation to a potential huge client you need to win. All of your competitors are going after the same account; whoever lands this account will become the industry leader. It's obviously critical that you hone your presentation with hours of practice. Most people are content with preparing for the best-case scenario—they work the script, slave over the slides and presentation, and tell themselves it's going to go great. They visualize their presentation, concluding with a standing ovation by the prospective clients and being handed a check—because that's what we're taught: to visualize everything going perfectly. But it should be the opposite. To be ultimately prepared, you don't plan for the best-case scenario; you plan for *every* scenario. What happens when you get in the boardroom and your projector doesn't work? What happens when you prepared to present to three people but you walk in and have an audience of thirty people? What happens when you finish and, instead of applause, everyone just looks puzzled? What are your answers when they challenge you with incredibly tough questions? Expecting adversity is about being ready for everything that could possibly come up.

The idea is to hope for the best but plan for the worst. If you are prepared for adversity, when it strikes (and it's going to strike), you can be confident in your preparation and ability to execute, regardless of circumstance.

CHAPTER 5

CONFIDENCE

★

When you have confidence, you can have a lot of fun. And when you have fun, you can do amazing things.

—JOE NAMATH

FRIDAY, JULY 22, 2016
STUBHUB CENTER, CARSON, CA

At any other competition in the world, an event modeled after Navy SEAL training would be enough for one day. But this is the CrossFit Games, and the athletes are far from done. They have just ninety minutes between the end of Murph and the start of the next event, but half of those minutes are not their own. Almost as soon as the last competitor crosses the finish line in the soccer stadium, the athletes are herded to the adjacent tennis stadium for their next event briefing. The flock of brightly colored, behatted competitors files over together, laughing and joking with one another. They receive the major details of the next event from Dave Castro on the floor of the tennis stadium, then are corralled back into a tunnel to review movement standards and scoring with head judge Adrian Bozman. Only after that are they released to go eat, recover, and begin warming up.

The next event is a strength test consisting of thirty squat cleans at ascending weight and descending reps.

EVENT 6:
Squat Clean Pyramid

For Time:
10 Squat Cleans (men 245 lb. / women 165 lb.), by 2:00
8 Squat Cleans (men 265 lb. / women 180 lb.), by 4:00
6 Squat Cleans (men 285 lb. / women 195 lb.), by 6:00
4 Squat Cleans (men 305 lb. / women 205 lb.), by 8:00
2 Squat Cleans (men 325 lb. / women 215 lb.), by 11:00

The competitors will progress, as fast as possible, through five stations of increasingly heavy weights. Even by Olympic weightlifting standards, the loading is hefty—the weight on the final barbell, for both the men and the women, would be enough to qualify an American middleweight for Weightlifting Nationals, and these athletes have to do twenty-eight repetitions as quickly as possible before attempting that final weight. Ostensibly, this is a strength test, but there's a twist—there are time cutoffs at each barbell after which athletes are not permitted to advance unless they have completed the prerequisite work, making "Squat Clean Pyramid" a power-endurance test as well as a strength test. Who can lift heavy when the heart rate is high?

I find Katrín and Cole back in the warm-up area, chatting with Sevan about the event. He asks them how they feel about it. "I prefer going long and lifting with a high heart rate rather than the one-rep-max things, so I'm excited about that," Katrín says. Cole bobs his head in agreement. "I like the work-capacity dynamic," he says. Listening to them, you'd think that they were about to go out and smash the event. They sound supremely confident. They *are* supremely confident.

But they're not going to smash this event. By normal standards, yes, Katrín and Cole are superhumanly strong. But compared to their peers at the Games, their strength numbers are merely average. They're under no illusions about this fact—they know that, not only are they not going to win, but they're going struggle in this event. So why do they sound so confident?

The answer lies in a definition of confidence that goes against conventional wisdom. People think confidence is the belief that you have the ability to win, or at least to compete with the best. But that's not what confidence is, or where it comes from. Confidence has nothing to do with outcome. It can't. Because I don't care how good you are, but in most sports you aren't going to "win" most of the time.

Last year, when Katrín won the CrossFit Games, she only won *one* event. One. Out of thirteen. She had five top-ten finishes, but she had even more finishes outside the top ten. If confidence came from winning, how could she ever be confident? Similarly, the greatest golf and tennis players of all time have one to two dozen major wins, but they compete in ten times that many tournaments, so they are losing much more than they are winning. The best hitters in baseball are successful three to four times out of ten. Michael Jordan was entrusted with taking the final game-winning shot fifty-one times in his NBA career, but missed twenty-six times.

Confidence doesn't come from knowing that you control the outcome of a given event or moment. It comes from knowing that you control your *response* to a given event. Confidence is about your competitive drive, your focus, positivity, perseverance, and grit, and whether you can maintain those characteristics when it matters most. Can you maintain the characteristics of a champion, regardless of what life throws at you? If you can—that's confidence.

Ohio State football coach Urban Meyer calls this the Success Equation:

$$E + R = O$$

$$EVENT + RESPONSE = OUTCOME$$

This equation teaches something very important about the way life works. We don't control the events in life, and we don't have direct control over the outcomes. The only thing we do have total control over is how we choose to respond. Successful people focus on the R part of the equation, while unsuccessful people tend to focus too much on the E part. Katrín understands this, which is why she's relaxed and confident as she warms up for Squat Clean Pyramid. She can't control the events that are thrown at her, but she has ultimate control over her responses to those events. She has a champion's understanding of confidence—her mindset is the same regardless of whether she's good or bad at an event.

As Bob Rotella explains, "Exceptional competitors understand that the primary competition is themselves. They understand that the biggest struggle is always the one within, the struggle to bring their best physical and mental self to the competition floor and maintain that presence until they cross the finish line." Katrín knows that the primary competition is the barbell, not the other women in her heat. If she can meet the challenge of the event, if she can master herself, she knows that she can be happy with wherever her finish lands her on the leaderboard. Her ability to maximize her potential regardless of the circumstances is where her confidence comes from.

It's a skill she's worked hard to develop. I know what Katrín's face looks like when she's about to enter events at the Games that play to her strengths. I know the look in her eye, her mannerisms, her approach, her posture—it's ultimate confidence. I also know what it looks like when other athletes get workouts that they don't like. Last year, Katrín was one of them.

Entering Event 8 of last year's CrossFit Games, Katrín had taken over first place on the leaderboard in the women's competition. Normally this is an exciting moment because you get to don the white leader's jersey. Much like the yellow jersey in the Tour de France, it signifies to the crowd that you are the one to watch, and that you are now the favorite to be crowned "Fittest on Earth."

Katrín was not excited to be in the lead. In fact, she freaked out and started to cry just moments before going onto the competition floor. Event 8 involved her nemesis, a big set of legless rope climbs right in the middle of the workout—the same legless rope climbs that kept her from making it to the Games in 2014. Katrín's fear was that all eyes would be on her, in the leader's jersey, as she epically failed once again, only this time on a much bigger stage. It was my job as a coach to get her confident again so she could perform to the peak of her potential.

I wasn't going to restore her confidence by pumping her up with motivational one-liners or empty promises that she could win. My job was to help her reframe the workout to where being successful would be manageable and within her control. I asked her if she thought she could do one rope climb. Just one. She nodded, and said she could do that. "Great," I told her. "After that one rope climb, imagine we are back in the gym training by ourselves like we do every Saturday." (We work on rope climbs every Saturday while training for the Games.) "Imagine," I told her, "that there are no CrossFit Games, there is no crowd, and there are no other competitors. Just you and me. Then ask yourself, 'When would Ben say I'm ready to do another rope climb?' When you think I'd say you're ready, jump up and do one more. If you can do two rope climbs, that is our win." She agreed that this was completely within her ability, and her confidence began to be restored. Within a few minutes she was smiling, laughing, and excited about the challenge ahead.

By lowering her expectations—not raising them like we are told to do—we were able to get her to perform at her peak potential. She ended up completing three full rope climbs before getting time-capped, and she came in fifteenth place out of forty athletes in that event. At the sound of the finishing buzzer, she turned to her judge. "I won," she said, grinning. Her judge glanced at the finish line, to the handful of women that had completed the full workout in the time requirement, then back to Katrín, "Um, honey," her judge began, gently. "Do you see those girls over there? They all finished ahead of you..." Katrín, still smiling, shook her head and looked at her meaningfully. "No," she said. "I *won*." Of course, Kat knew she hadn't really won the workout. What she meant was that it didn't matter what the leaderboard said. She was able to control her response and deliver the absolute best performance she was capable of.

Katrín faces a similar situation now, as she waits on the stairs outside the tennis stadium for her heat to start.

She knows she isn't going to win Squat Clean Pyramid, and that there are two potential responses in the face of this challenge.

The first one is what most people do when faced with adversity—focus on external factors. They start a negative monologue in their heads: *The other girls are so much stronger than me. What if I can't lift the last barbell? What's going to happen to my position on the leaderboard? I can predict where I am going to finish by counting the number of girls with bigger strength numbers than me.*

The other option is to realize the event itself is outside of her control and to ignore the other women completely, knowing that their performances have no bearing on her ability to deliver her own best effort.

The second approach is the correct one, but it's easier said than done. The heats are organized by position on the leaderboard, so Katrín, who is sitting in seventh, will be lifting alongside some of the strongest women in CrossFit. Being confident in the warm-up area is one thing, but holding on to it and executing your game plan in the heat of battle, amid thousands of screaming fans, is quite another.

The women jog down the stadium stairs into the bowl of the tennis court and line up in front of a long row of barbells. The clock starts, and the field races out to the first station. Unsurprisingly, Australian powerhouse Kara Webb jumps out to an early lead, completing ten reps at 165 pounds in just twenty-five seconds. The other top women—Brooke Wells, Tia-Clair Toomey, and Sara Sigmundsdóttir—try and chase her down. Katrín hangs back, moving her barbell more deliberately. Only a few of the women can keep up with Webb's blistering pace. Wells and Toomey clear the final barbells with relative ease and leap onto the finish platform shortly after Webb.

At this point, Katrín and Sara Sigmundsdóttir are the only two heavyweights left out on the floor. Sara, like Katrín, is one of the top competitors in the sport. She is stronger than Katrín and is one of the favorites to win the Games this year. However, she arrives at the final barbell and fails her first rep. She tries again a few seconds later to the same effect. Meanwhile, Katrín has caught up to her—she makes the first rep at 205, then rolls her bar forward next to Sara's.

The two women set up at the same time. Both get under the weight but can't stand it up. Frustrated, Sara readjusts her lifting belt and quickly loads up for another attempt. She fails again. Katrín gives herself a moment to regain her composure—she walks ten feet behind her, slaps her legs, and lets out a yell. I know that yell—"*Koma!*"—which is "*Come on!*" in Icelandic. A good sign. She strides back up to the barbell, twists her feet into the ground, grips the bar, and jumps and shrugs powerfully. She catches it high on her shoulders, and this time stands it up. She leaps, ecstatic, onto the finish platform and is joined thirty seconds later by Sara.

Katrín takes fifteenth in the event, which, considering we weren't sure if she would even be able to lift the final weight, is a huge victory. In an event where she could have placed anywhere from fifteenth to twenty-fifth, her finish represents her best-case scenario. The same cannot be said of Sara Sigmundsdóttir. Sara is a considerably stronger athlete than Katrín, and would be the favorite in any head-to-head strength test on paper. But by trying to keep up with Kara Webb's scorching pace early on, she compromised her ability to maximize her potential—her seventeenth place finish, while only two places below Katrín, is well below what I suspect she's capable of.

It's a powerful example of the critical role confidence plays at the highest levels. True confidence is being secure in the knowledge that fully committing to training and competing with excellence is enough, even if that excellence doesn't produce victories. That's it. It's knowing that you don't need to be winning all the time, that you are still okay if you aren't winning at halftime, that it's okay if the opposing team goes on a hot streak, and that the season isn't over if you lose a game or two. Ultimate confidence is the understanding that you simply need to find a way to give your best at every moment and every opportunity in order to measure up to your own standard of success. It's an approach I modeled after a mantra coined by Joe Friel, a top triathlon coach: "Think like a bumblebee, train like a racehorse."

Racehorses are special. They're not like just any other horse—they're elite athletes, and they know it. They train with heart monitors, they do interval workouts, they have coaches and massage therapists, they eat a special diet, and they have recovery protocols. It sounds like I'm describing a human athlete, and I very well could be, because top racehorses and top human athletes are similar in just about every way but one. That one difference is crucial, and it gives racehorses a huge advantage over us: racehorses can't think for themselves.

I get it; that doesn't sound like an advantage. But think about it: racehorses are incapable of second-guessing their coaches, overanalyzing their performance, or logging junk miles. They're unable to sandbag a workout if they're not feeling up for training on a particular day. They don't look at the other racehorses and compare themselves, or wonder if they're with the right coach and training program. On race day, they don't walk by the stalls of their competitors and think, *Holy crap, look at the legs on him! How am I going to compete with that?*

Racehorses just perform. They can't second-guess anything, and they have no biological choice but to have a laser focus on the task at hand. They're able to do what we try to get our human athletes to do, as naturally as breathing. When they win, they don't change anything about their routine, and they aren't fundamentally changed. The next day is just another training day because winning (or losing) is part of the process, not the endpoint.

The comparison aspect I mentioned is particularly damaging to athletes, and its absence is the part of the racehorse's mind I most wish I could download into the minds of the athletes I train. In our sport, especially, comparison is *everywhere*, and it's ridiculously hard to avoid. CrossFit athletes are social media stars, and all year, every day, they're posting their training, lifts, and personal records for their hundreds of thousands of followers to see. When the Games season rolls out, athletes have to post their scores to an online leaderboard week by week. It's an immense distraction. How can you *not* be tempted to check how your score stacks up? How can you *not* wonder if your competition is getting stronger, faster, and more sharply skilled than you?

As much as is humanly possible, I have my athletes shut it all out. They don't post their workouts to Instagram, and they don't so much as glance at the leaderboard. The knowledge that one of your biggest rivals crushed a workout that was tough for you could cause you to second-guess your training, your program, and your process. Questions and doubt may start careening through your head. Or perhaps you excelled in a workout and shot to the top of the leaderboard, and so you allow yourself to be lulled into a false sense of security and take your foot off the pedal, only to let your competitors catch up.

Racehorses aren't biologically capable of understanding what their competitors are doing. They're completely focused on themselves. That's where I want my athletes. If an athlete's goal is to beat their competitor, then, by definition, they're not reaching their full potential—they're simply clearing the bar of the next guy's potential.

Bumblebees are the other side of the confidence coin. Bumblebees are physically improbable creatures that somehow exist and fly around contrary to every physical law that states they shouldn't be able to. They're relatively huge, heavy, furry animals, with proportionally tiny wings. Before anyone took the time to actually figure out how bumblebees stay in the air, the popular folklore saying was (and actually, still is): "According to physics, bumblebees can't fly, but nobody ever explained physics to bumblebees, so they fly around anyway." Where this relates to the athlete mindset is that the bumblebee is the definition of confident: it knows that flying is what it should be doing; so, contrary to the natural laws of the world, it keeps on doing exactly what it believes it is capable of doing.

As humans, we have the have the ability to think on a deeper level. In the boardroom, or in a relationship, careful, meticulous thought brings you success; but in sports, this works against us. Out on the field, it's a disaster. On the field, in order to win, you need to be 100 percent confident that you are where you're supposed to be, and 100 percent focused on the task in front of you. You need to be in the "zone"—in the place where your subconscious mind takes over and *thinking* stops. Thinking is slow. We want athletes to be automatic.

Obviously, we can't be racehorses and bumblebees at all times, which is part of the reason I work so hard with my athletes to build their mindset *before* they step out onto the competition floor. We work every day to construct pathways in the brain that will keep them focused on the process and dedicated to the work even when circumstances and conditions are incredibly distracting. Confidence happens when you make the most challenging keys to success part of the daily grind and stick with the character traits unwaveringly.

Additionally, confidence is a character trait that develops from defining success in terms that can be controlled by the athlete. In fact, one of the most important components of building my athletes' mindsets is coming up with a definition of success that is *not* tied to the result they're after. Most people would look at Katrín and define success for her as winning the Games twice. What happens, then, if she doesn't win? Is she a failure? Tying success or failure to one single point in time, one event over which you really don't have much control of the circumstances, sets you up for unavoidable failure because there's no way anyone can win every single time.

As an exercise, I ask my athletes what success means to them, and ask them to write it down, share it with me, and then display it somewhere they will see it every day—like on a bathroom mirror or on their fridge. Here's Katrín's definition of success:

> *Success to me is giving full effort knowing that was the best I was capable of. That said, full effort means nothing if day-to-day preparation was not all I had. Success to me is giving everything I have into each and every day, each and every moment; training, recovery, family, friends,*

giving back, inspiring, loving what I do. Then, come game time, give full effort, knowing I am the best I am capable of becoming.

Notice that there's nothing in there about winning, nothing about scores, nothing about personal records. Actually, since we began working together, we've never talked about winning the CrossFit Games. Never once has the subject been uttered.

We choose to focus on what's inside our control, and what we can control is exactly what she defined as success. It's what we can focus on this day, this hour, this minute. We can work into each and every moment with every ounce of effort and personal grit we can muster. In doing that, we're truly successful in each moment. Results, when you live and work that way, are a foregone conclusion.

The flip side, the opposite mindset, would put us in a place where success would be determined by Katrín's performance during one single week in July. The preceding fifty-one weeks are just hoping we can make success happen, and we have no idea where we stand. Her entire year, and her whole measure of value, riding on five days in July is not a great way to experience your best. The pressure of those five days would be mentally insurmountable. For Katrín, the pressure she feels when faced with an event at the Games that's not in her wheelhouse, like the Squat Clean Pyramid, is exactly the same as the pressure of any other day. She simply gives all she has, in each and every moment.

CHAPTER 6

MAXIMIZING MINUTES

★

Now is everything you have to work with. When you live it fully, it is more than enough.

—RALPH MARSTON

FRIDAY, JULY 22, 2016
STUBHUB CENTER, CARSON, CA

Day 3 of competition is still not over. There is one (still unknown) event remaining, which will take place under the lights of the tennis stadium later tonight.

Friday Night Lights is a hallowed tradition at the Cross-Fit Games. The fans live for it—it's what they've come for—but no one loves Friday Night Lights more than the competitors. "The tennis stadium is where magic happens," Katrín once said, matter-of-factly. She's not wrong; the StubHub tennis stadium has a magical energy to it. Though it seats ten thousand people, it feels oddly intimate, as though all ten thousand are on the floor next to you. Games athletes thrive on this floor; they equate it to being gladiators in the Colosseum. Cole, who played Division I football in front of hundreds of thousands of fans, says it's the most electrifying environment he has ever been in.

Around 3:00 p.m., Dave summons the athletes to the floor of the currently empty tennis stadium to reveal tonight's event. He reminds us that last year, the Games let the fans help decide the Friday Night Lights event. They could choose between two variations of a classic CrossFit benchmark workout, "DT" (a triplet of deadlifts, hang power cleans, and push jerks): a much heavier version (205 lb. for men and 145 lb. for women, instead of the customary 155 lb. and 105 lb.) or a much longer version (ten rounds instead of five). The fans voted in favor of Heavy DT.

By choosing Heavy DT in 2015, Dave says, the fans unknowingly locked in Double DT for 2016. Katrín, who is standing with Cole, lets out a yelp when Dave announces this and pounds Cole's shoulder gleefully. This does not go unnoticed by Sevan Matossian, the documentarian. He meets up with us in the warm-up area after the event briefing and asks about it. "Is this something you practice a lot?" Katrín plays coy, but I tell him the truth—two weeks ago we practiced "Murph" in training then followed it up with "Double DT." Katrín bursts out laughing and looks at me like I'm a wizard.

I'm not a wizard. The CrossFit Games are unknown and unknowable, yes, and it's impossible to guess the specifics of the events. But the test itself is well understood, so it's possible to use information to predict, with some degree of accuracy, the kinds of things that might show up. In order to find the world's fittest athletes, you have to test for certain things. You have to know how fast someone is in a very short time domain, like sprinting. You have to know how strong someone is, so there has to be some heavy lifting. You have to find out who has great endurance—trail runs, triathlons, and so on. You have to test work capacity in long, medium, and short time domains with varied movements.

Murph is a long body-weight workout. The counterbalance to that is a short time domain involving a barbell. And since Double DT was left on the table last year, it wasn't a stretch to assume it might be in play this year. It wasn't a sure thing, but we practiced and strategized for it.

EVENT 7:
Double DT

10 Rounds:
12 Deadlifts (men 155 lb. / women 105 lb.)
9 Hang Power Cleans (men 155 lb. / women 105 lb.)
6 Push Jerks (men 155 lb. / women 105 lb.)

As the sun starts to sink, Katrín and I talk through our game plan in the warm-up area. "The idea is not to go out guns blazing," I tell her. "Be a smart, mature athlete." Katrín, who can cycle a moderate-weight barbell as well as anyone in the sport, amends this slightly. "Guns blazing," she says, "but calm and relaxed." I nod. "Show me strong; show me smart."

Athlete Control arrives to collect the women for heat check-ins, so I give Kat a hug, and then O'Keefe and I head over to find our seats in the tennis stadium. As spectating goes, it doesn't get better than Friday Night Lights at the CrossFit Games. The air is filled with a buzzing sound of fans rushing to their seats, hurrying to get settled; they don't want to miss a minute of what's coming.

The MC's voice booms over the mic, and the top-ranked heat of women jog down the stairs amid roaring cheers. They take their places on the starting mats and wait for the starting beep.

One minute in, I know Katrín is going to win this event. The other girls blitz through the first round, but Katrín lets them go. She's moving the barbell methodically, completely oblivious to the other women, the crowd, and the announcers. In the fifth round, she starts picking people off. She passes one girl, then another. She catches the leaders in round seven, and by round eight she's out in front. Everything is identical to her first round—her movements, facial expression, and strategy are exactly the same in round nine as they were in round one. Practically everyone is failing reps and taking longer breaks, but Katrín is just hitting her stride; her hang power cleans, which looked slow in the first five rounds, now look terrifyingly fast. She jumps up on the finish platform twenty seconds before second-place finisher Brooke Wells.

Later, commentator Sean Woodland observes, "Katrín may not be the most physically gifted athlete in the field, but what's between her ears made the difference in that event." His point is well taken: Hard work is incredibly important—you can't get to or stay at the elite level without it. But once you're there, hard work is not enough. To continue to rise, you have to work smarter, more efficiently, and more strategically. Malcolm Gladwell alludes to this concept in his book *Outliers*. Gladwell makes a compelling case for what he calls "The 10,000 Hour Rule"—that is, that you need ten thousand hours of practice to become world-class at anything.

Gladwell's 10,000 Hour Rule is based on a study conducted by the psychologist K. Anders Ericsson in the 1990s at Berlin's elite Academy of Music:

> With the help of the Academy's professors, they divided the school's violinists into three groups. In the first group were the stars, the students with the potential to become world-class soloists. In the second were those judged to be merely "good." In the third were students who were unlikely to ever play professionally and who intended to be music teachers in the public school system. All of the violinists were then asked the same question: over the course of your entire career, ever since you first picked up the violin, how many hours have you practiced?
>
> Everyone from all three groups started playing at roughly the same age, around five years old. In those first few years, everyone practiced roughly the same amount, about two or three hours a week. But when

the students were around the age of eight, real differences started to emerge. The students who would end up the best in their class began to practice more than everyone else: six hours a week by age nine, eight hours a week by age twelve, sixteen hours a week by age fourteen, and up and up, until by the age of twenty they were practicing well over thirty hours a week. In fact, by the age of twenty, the elite performers had each totaled ten thousand hours of practice. By contrast, the merely good students had totaled eight thousand hours, and the future music teachers had totaled just over four thousand hours.

Ericsson and his colleagues then compared amateur pianists with professional pianists. The same pattern emerged. The amateurs never practiced more than about three hours a week over the course of their childhood, and by the age of twenty they had totaled two thousand hours of practice. The professionals, on the other hand, steadily increased their practice time every year, until by the age of twenty they, like the violinists, had reached ten thousand hours.

"The emerging picture from such studies is that ten thousand hours of practice is required to achieve the level of mastery associated with being a world-class expert—in anything," writes neurologist Daniel Levitin. "In study after study, of composers, basketball players, fiction writers, ice skaters, concert pianists, chess players, master criminals, and what have you, this number comes up again and again. Of course, this doesn't address why some people get more out of their practice sessions than others do. But no one has yet found a case in which true world-class expertise was accomplished in less time. It seems that it takes the brain this long to assimilate all that it needs to know to achieve true mastery."

The 10,000 Hour Rule, however, misses an important nuance. Extensive experience is necessary to reach very high levels of performance; however, extensive experience does not invariably lead to expert levels of achievement. "Some types of experience, such as merely executing proficiently during routine work, may not lead to further improvement," writes Ericsson. "After a certain point, further improvement depends on deliberate efforts to change particular aspects of performance."

In other words, just accruing ten thousand hours at something will not make you world-class; for example, I have been driving for more than twenty years, but I'm no more qualified to be an Indianapolis 500 driver than my seventeen-year-old daughter. There's nothing magical about ten thousand hours—the magic lies in *how* those hours are spent.

You need a particular kind of practice—what psychologists call "deliberate practice"—to develop expertise. When most people practice, they focus on the things they already know how to do. Deliberate practice, Ericsson writes, is different. It involves stepping outside your comfort zone and trying activities beyond your current abilities. It entails considerable, specific, and sustained efforts to do something you can't do well—or even at all. Research across domains shows that it is only by working at what you can't do that you turn into the expert you want to become.

Deliberate practice can be characterized by the following four elements:

1. It's designed specifically to improve performance.
2. It is repeated a lot.
3. Feedback on results is continuously available.
4. It's highly demanding mentally, and not necessarily or particularly enjoyable, because it means you are focusing on improving areas in your performance that are not satisfactory.

The requirement for concentration is what sets deliberate practice apart from both mindless routine performance and playful engagement. The takeaway here is that while hard work is instrumental to success, it's not enough.

Obviously, the CrossFit Games does not hand out medals based on who spent the most time in the gym. Katrín didn't win the Games last year because she logged more hours in the gym than all the other women. She won the Games because of the *quality* of those hours.

I coach my athletes to maximize every minute of every day. Katrín, Mat, and Cole don't just go through the motions, because at the elite level, it's not enough just to show up. If the goal is to get better every single day, you have to make every moment you're practicing the best you're possibly capable of.

Right now, in this minute, in these sixty seconds, what is it you should be doing to maximize your capabilities and results? Right now, should you be warming up? Are you moving through your warm-up with the most attention, the most care and effort, that you can bring to it? Right now, should you be training—and are you giving your training your all? Should you be recovering, eating, or sleeping? Are you giving each minute the respect it deserves? Every minute of your day is a building block that goes toward creating your success, your measure of excellence. Every minute deserves your utmost attention and commitment.

This kind of deliberate practice is the difference between

wildly successful people and everyone else. And yet, deliberate practice is uncommonly rare; the average person does not practice like this, much less sustain it over a ten-year period. Why not?

Because it's *hard*.

Becoming world-class at something takes an extraordinary amount of work. As Gladwell illustrates, it takes a minimum of ten years of practice before you can expect to start achieving at an elite level. Along the way, you have to practice like you're possessed. The kind of deliberate practice that leads to success takes a level of commitment, dedication, patience, focus, grit, and resilience that is impossible without an essential ingredient.

Passion.

The only way you can dedicate yourself completely to something—to be *all in*, every single day, leaving nothing on the table—is if you're passionate about it. You have to *love* it. The people who make it to the top—whether they're musicians, athletes, or CEOs—are addicted to their calling. They jump out of bed every morning excited about doing their work. Not that they consider it work; they're the ones who'd be doing whatever it is they love, even if they weren't being paid.

It's possible to be very good at something you're not passionate about. But it makes everything harder. The daily grind—the deliberate practice—is exhausting for the CEO who lacks passion for his career. For the entrepreneur who loves his job, the daily grind is fun. It's exciting. If he could be doing anything in the world, this would be it. As Bob Rotella says, "Sticking with something you love is like biking downhill. Sticking with something you don't love is like biking uphill."

When drive faces off with passion, it's no contest.

Nowhere is there a better example of this than the Wright brothers. One of my favorite TED Talks is a lecture by Simon Sinek called "How Great Leaders Inspire Action."* In it, he tells the little-known story of Samuel Pierpont Langley: "Back in the early twentieth century, the pursuit of powered man flight was like the dot-com of the day—everybody was trying it." Samuel Pierpont Langley had, by almost every metric, everything he needed to succeed. He was funded by the US government and had an unlimited budget. "He held a seat at Harvard and worked at the Smithsonian and was extremely well connected; he knew all the big minds of the day. He hired the best minds money could find and the market conditions

***

* Simon Sinek, "How Great Leaders Inspire Action," Ted Talk, September 2009, https://www.ted.com/talks/simon_sinek_how_great_leaders_inspire_action.

were fantastic. The *New York Times* followed him around everywhere, and everyone was rooting for Langley."

Sinek continues: "A few hundred miles away, in Dayton, Ohio, Orville and Wilbur Wright had none of what we consider to be the recipe for success. They had no money; they paid for their dream with the proceeds from their bicycle shop. Not a single person on the Wright brothers' team had a college education, including Orville and Wilbur; and the *New York Times* followed them around nowhere."

So why have we never heard of Samuel Pierpont Langley, whereas the Wright Brothers are a household name?

Sinek explains that Orville and Wilbur Wright were motivated by a cause, while Langley was motivated by a result. The Wright Brothers had a purpose, a larger *why*. "They believed that if they could figure out this flying machine, it would change the course of the world." Langley, who did not share their enthusiasm for flight, was driven only by the prospect of wealth and fame. The result? "The people who believed in the Wright brothers' dream worked with them with blood and sweat and tears." Langley's team "just worked for the paycheck." When the Wright brothers took flight on December 17, 1903, Langley quit. He could have marveled over their discovery and sought to improve upon their technology, but he didn't. As Sinek says, "He wasn't first, he didn't get rich, he didn't get famous, so he quit."

The truth is, for all his funding and resources, Langley never stood a chance. Passion will outperform drive every time, because passion breeds a bulletproof level of resilience. And if you're trying to be the best at something—if you're trying to change the world—you're going to need it, because it's going to be incredibly hard. Passion is the antidote to setbacks, disadvantage, ridicule, and bad luck—all of which you're going to encounter repeatedly if you're chasing excellence. Passion allows you to persevere when any other sane person would quit.

To the outside world, it looks like super-high-achieving performers are giving up everything that really matters in life. Katrín is a poignant example. Most twenty-four-year-old girls have jobs, friends, and an active social schedule. They have boyfriends, they go to parties, they watch Netflix, and eat pizza. Katrín doesn't do anything that normal girls her age do. She wakes up every morning and reads books about mindset. She spends seven hours in the gym, then spends the remaining hours seeing bodywork specialists, prepping her nutrition, and following recovery protocols. It's a laser-focused life, and it seems like a huge sacrifice to those of us wanting to live in balance. From time to time, someone will point this out to her. Her response is always the same. "I'm not sacrificing anything," she says. "I love what I'm doing. If you gave me the choice of anything in the world to do, I'd do exactly this."

Passion is one of the first things I look for when bringing on a new athlete. It's the character trait that enables all the other character traits that are so critical to success at the elite level—hunger, commitment, dedication, grit, perseverance, resilience, and patience. Katrín's passion for being the fittest in the world and her genuine love of training has made her an unstoppable force. As she stands on the finish mat below me, smiling radiantly, it's written all over her face.

I find Katrín outside the stadium after DT. It's been a long day of competition, but our workday isn't over yet—we still have hours of recovery ahead of us. As we're walking, Sevan and his camera find us again. He falls into step with us, looking determined, and begins peppering Kat with questions. Unselfconsciously candid as always, he observes to Katrín that she seems closer to her coach than most people. She glances at me, then nods. "I am," she says. "The way that he coaches, his approach to training, fits with me. He focuses on character rather than results. Since I've been working with him, he hasn't just taught me how to be a better athlete and how to work hard. He's made me a better person. We focus on all those characteristics day in and day out, and it's made a big difference."

It's the first time I've heard Katrín talk analytically about our methodology. I watch her as she talks. Her eyes say that she's figured something out, something essential. For all her success so far, I begin to feel as though this is just the beginning for her.

CHAPTER 7

THE PROCESS

★

Only those who have the patience to do things perfectly will acquire the skills to do difficult things easily.

—FRIEDRICH SCHILLER

SATURDAY, JULY 23, 2016
STUBHUB CENTER, CARSON, CA

I'm strolling around in Vendor Village, at large for an hour while Katrín, Mat, and Cole attend an athlete briefing. Erected in the sprawling east parking lot of the Stub-Hub Center, Vendor Village is like a CrossFit bazaar. It seems as if every company that manufactures CrossFit-related merchandise is here, hawking their wares. You can find practically anything in Vendor Village, from the functional—apparel, gym equipment, backpacks, straw banana hats, supplements; to the less functional—tactical vests, children's toy barbells, temporary tattoos; to the obscure—hand callus razors, silicone wedding rings. All I want is a KillCliff recovery drink, but the sheer number of vendor tents and people is disorienting. With the start of individual competition still hours away, this is clearly the place to be—it seems that all ten thousand spectators are down here reveling in the fitness festival that is the CrossFit Games.

Back up in the StubHub complex, my athletes are standing together in the warm-up area, like high school students before class. Mat, who has an engineering degree from the University of Vermont, is giving Katrín and Cole a physics lesson prior to the start of the next event, Climbing Snail. Since the first time the athletes will get to push the hay-bale-esque Snails will be out on the competition floor, much of the preparation for this event is theoretical. When I meet up with them, Mat, looking oddly professorial, is making a circle with his hands. The power needs to go into the middle of the circle, he tells us. "When you're pushing a circle, all the force has to go into the middle. You have to be thinking about driving it forward; you're not lifting it or driving it down." Hopefully he's right.

EVENT 8:
Climbing Snail

3 Rounds:
500 m Berm Run
2 Rope Climbs
40' Snail Push
2 Rope Climbs

The odd-object events always produce a lot of creativity in the athlete warm-up area. Obviously, there are no Snails lying around, so all the coaches and athletes comb through the available equipment and fashion, with varying degrees of success, things that might resemble one. I stack a bunch of weights on a plyo box and have Katrín push it around the floor, while Mat and Cole push O'Keefe around on a GHD sit-up machine.

The women are up first, and Athlete Control summons them over the loudspeaker to the staging area. As Katrín trots off to check in, I'm encouraged. She is worlds more positive than she was before last year's rope-climb event. I can tell she's tense, but she's also confident—I can see the confidence shining from her eyes. Unlike last year, I don't have to give her a speech to redefine her expectations, refuel her confidence, or reiterate what competitive excellence looks like. She's internalized it—she knows exactly what she's capable of and exactly what she needs to do.

O'Keefe and I make what feels like our 157th walk from the warm-up area to the StubHub concourse to take our seats in the infernal soccer stadium. It's way hotter today than it was yesterday; it was 82 degrees during Murph yesterday, but it's 97 degrees now. It's so hot that the equipment team is covering the Snails with tarps between heats so that the scorching rubber doesn't melt the athletes' hands off. O'Keefe, who is incurably Irish, is turning as red as the Snails on the field.

Katrín's heat jogs out, and we watch as she delivers her best CrossFit Games performance ever. Kat knows it too—she runs across the finish line with both hands in the air and for a full five minutes is physically incapable of not smiling. I find her back in the warm-up area after, glowing like she ate a flashlight. "This is the happiest I've ever been," she tells me. She says it casually, almost in passing, but the comment speaks volumes about her mindset. Here is a woman who has won the CrossFit Games—the highest achievement in our sport—telling me that taking sixth in a workout is the happiest she's ever felt. Why? She didn't win the event. She's not even on top of the leaderboard; after eight events, she's still sitting in third. So why is she so incandescently happy?

Because Katrín, more than anyone I've ever met or coached, has bought into the process. "The process" is a term that's been popularized by University of Alabama football coach Nick Saban. Alabama, of course, is the gold standard of college football—the Crimson Tide has won four of the last six national championships, sustaining a caliber of success that's unparalleled in the modern era. Saban doesn't focus on what every other coach focuses on, or at least not the *way* they do. He teaches the process:

> Don't think about winning the SEC Championship. Don't think about the national championship. Think about what you need to do in this drill, on this play, in this moment. That's the process: Let's think about what we can do today, the task at hand.

The process is about focusing on the steps to success rather than worrying about the result. It's an ethos that high achievers have in common, and it forms the crux of how I coach my athletes. Katrín and I never talk about winning the CrossFit Games. Instead, we focus on creating the right thoughts, habits, and priorities, with the belief that those are the things that lead to success. As Bob Knight, the famous basketball coach, used to tell his team, "Do what has to be done, as well as it can be done. Then do it that way all the time."

At its heart, the process is the single-minded emphasis of preparation above all else. In practice, this is very mundane—the process is many things, but glamorous is not one of them.

The most fundamental movement in our sport is called the air squat. There's no weight, no barbell; you simply squat down until your thighs are below parallel, and stand back up. It's not a movement that any Games athlete thinks twice about. When I first started working with Katrín, she was an athlete who'd made it to the Games twice, yet we worked on her air squat as our focus for a month and a half. Kat was a gymnast as a teenager, so she has an overly flexible spine and a propensity to hyperextend her back in an arch. When she does that, she loses stability in her core; basically, her abs stop firing. So, we made perfecting her air squat our top priority. For the first six weeks of working together, we repeatedly and incessantly performed, practiced, critiqued, and refined the least sexy movement in our sport.

This past year, after she won the Games, we did the same thing. Throughout the competition, I'd seen so many things in her movements that could be improved. She was excellent, obviously—she'd won, after all—but she wasn't perfect. On her first day back in the gym, we had a conversation, and I told her we were going to rebuild her, step by boring step.

We started with the muscle-up, an advanced, but fundamental movement in our sport. Muscle-ups are a milestone achievement in the life of a normal CrossFitter; getting your first one is something you work at for months, or years, and you never forget when you finally launch yourself up onto the rings. For the elite athletes, it's a movement that must be mastered and owned because, when competing at the highest level, the expectation is that you'll be doing dozens of them in a competitive event. At the time, Katrín could knock out an underwhelming six in a row. Instead of continually pushing her limits through threshold or volume training, both of which are exciting, I had her stop doing them entirely for ninety days. We began her new program by repeatedly performing just the very beginning of the movement, the kip swing. No pulling, no getting up on the rings, no dip out—just swinging with her arms straight, over and over. After three months of this, I had her add the next piece of the movement: pulling up onto the rings. We did that for another month. We continued like this, in monthly increments, doing just one perfect muscle-up a day for thirty days. Then we increased it to two, then three. I made her take big breaks between sets, and never programmed muscle-ups into a workout. It was six months before I put them back into a workout and, when I did, she was only allowed to do one at a time—no cycling reps. Each one had to be perfect. If they weren't what we wanted them to look like, we stopped the workout and got them back to where we wanted them to be.

This is the process—acknowledging where you are, identifying where you want to be, and breaking it down into pieces. Excellence is a matter of steps. Excel at this one, then that one, and then the one after that.

The process is simple, but it's not easy. Most people don't have the character traits necessary to fully commit to it. To have this level of dedication, to be able to activate the process and live it, you have to have the right character traits. That's why when I coach my athletes, I start by developing the human being first—I have to build humans with a high level of resiliency, patience, dedication, humility, and hunger. Once those traits are developed, we can start to follow the process. When character and process are both in place, the results will take care of themselves.

Nutrition is an area where underdeveloped character frequently impacts the process. Even at the highest level of athletics, there are always a few athletes who aren't as lean as they should be. They pass it off as genetics, or say, "It's just the way my body takes shape—I eat clean and train hard." But either they're deflecting, or they truly don't know that a higher level of dedication to their nutrition will make a huge difference in their ability to perform at their craft. Katrín's first two years at the Games are proof. She was in the "eat clean, train hard" camp, and didn't drill down into details with her diet the way a champion does. She was athletic and fit, but she didn't have the physique of an elite champion, and she didn't look anything like she does now.

In a sport where you have to be ready for absolutely any task, and you know body-weight skills are going to be involved, every single ounce of body weight makes a difference. If you weren't working with your body, but were working with a machine—no biases, no wants or desires, no temptations, just fuel in and performance out—what would you feed that machine? How would you train it? How would you rest it? That's the approach I take with my athletes. How can we squeeze every last bit of efficiency and work capacity out of the machines that are their bodies?

Today, Katrín's nutrition is dialed in to the nth degree. She weighs and measures every macronutrient that goes into her body. "Cheat meals" are limited to two or three per year (and they aren't what you and I would consider cheating). She's so dedicated to the process that she brings her own food in Tupperware to restaurants when she goes out to eat with friends. Is her rigid adherence to nutrition the reason she's successful? By itself, no. It's one of many small areas that combine to move the needle in a big way.

In management, this is known as the "aggregation of marginal gains." In a recent article, James Clear described how Dave Brailsford used this concept to revive Great Britain's ailing professional cycling team. As the new director of British cycling's Team Sky, Brailsford set about improving everything the team did by 1 percent, believing that those small gains would add up to remarkable improvement.

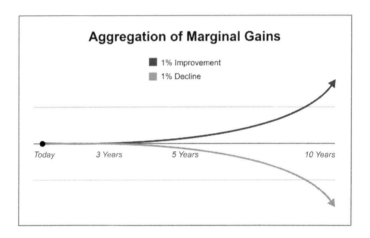

He started by optimizing the obvious: the nutrition of riders, their weekly training program, the ergonomics of the bike seat, and the weight of the tires. But Brailsford and his team didn't stop there. They searched for 1 percent improvements in tiny areas that were overlooked by almost everyone else—discovering the pillow that offered the best sleep and taking it with them to hotels, testing for the most effective type of massage gel, and teaching riders the best way to wash their hands to avoid infection. They searched for 1 percent improvements everywhere.

Brailsford believed that if they could successfully execute this strategy, Team Sky would be in a position to win the Tour de France in five years' time.

He was wrong—they won it in three years. Then won it again the year after that. Today, Team Sky has won four of the last five Tour de France events.

Take a look at the chart again. The most compelling takeaway is the time over which the 1 percents begin to make a difference. Day to day, small improvements don't make a difference. On the chart, they're indistinguishable from small declines. It's not until around year three that a gap begins to appear. From there, though, the differences begin diverging at a much faster rate. By year ten, the small daily improvements have added up; the line is well above where it started and leagues above the line representing the small daily declines.

This is what the process is all about—habits. We are the sum of what we repeatedly do; we're totally composed of the smallest details in our day. Katrín doesn't win because she's inhuman or a genetic freak. She's a talented person who has dedicated herself to the tiniest habits, day in and day out. The people who are the first in and the last to leave, and who commit every moment of the time in between to the pursuit of excellence, are the ones who end up on top.

Ray Allen is a top NBA player who has won two championships, one with the Boston Celtics and one with the Miami Heat. In a fantastic article, "Letter to My Younger Self," he writes to himself as a thirteen-year-old. Within the letter, he tells himself:

> You'll put up more than 26,000 shots in your career. Almost six out of 10 won't even go in. I told you this game was a sonofabitch. Don't worry, though. A successful man is built of 1,000 failures. Or in your case, 14,000 misses. You'll win a championship in Boston. You'll win another in Miami. The personalities on those two teams will be different, but both teams will have the same thing in common: habits. Boring old habits. I know you want me to let you in on some big secret to success in the NBA. The secret is there is no secret. It's just boring old habits.

> In every locker room you'll ever be in, everybody will say all the right things. Everybody says they're willing to sacrifice whatever it takes to win a title. But this game isn't a movie. It's not about being the man in the

fourth quarter. It's not about talk. It's getting in your work every single day, when nobody is watching. Kevin Garnett, Paul Pierce, LeBron James, Dwyane Wade. The men who you are going to win championships with are all going to be very different people. What makes them champions is the boring old habits that nobody sees. They compete to see who can be the first to get to the gym and the last to leave.

I started working with Katrín after the 2014 season, when she missed qualifying for the CrossFit Games. When the 2015 season started, she had one goal: make it back to the Games. She was willing to do anything to make it happen, so she committed herself completely and totally to the process. She left her family back in Iceland and moved across an ocean to train with me in Boston with zero distractions and total focus. She maximized her nutrition and left no stone unturned. She prioritized her sleep and recovery every single day. She warmed up every morning with the kind of attention and care most people reserve for game day. When training, she focused on giving her absolute best effort to the task at hand, whatever it was. She dedicated herself so completely to the process that something extraordinary happened. She didn't just make it back to the Games—she *won* them.

Following back-to-back second-place finishes at the 2014

and 2015 Games, Mat leveled up his own dedication to the process. After winning the 2016 East Regional with the most dominant performance in our sport's history, someone asked him what the difference was. "I've stopped traveling as much during competition season," he said. "I'm staying home. I want to keep in my routine so I can tap the potential out of every single day. I don't want to be taken out of my environment—I don't want to have to change my sleep schedule for three days at a time, or change my diet for a couple days. I want to just stay where I know I'm comfortable, where I know I can have my training routine."

Mat and Katrín have figured out the secret: that there is no secret. The process is about doing your job to the best of your ability, and Katrín and Mat wield it like a weapon. Do they want to win the CrossFit Games? Absolutely. But we don't talk about it, and we certainly don't make it a goal. Because what's more important to success than a bold and courageous goal is developing a system—a process—to get there.

Bill Belichick, coach of the New England Patriots, lives this better than anyone. In press conferences, he routinely frustrates reporters by delivering monotone, process-minded responses. When asked at the beginning of the 2016 season if the goal was to win another Super Bowl, he said:

That's too far away. The goal right now is to put a good and competitive team together. Then the goal would be to have our team to compete and work the way it needs to work to have a good spring, then to have a good training camp, and then to be ready for the start of the season. We can only control what we can control in the short term.

There's so much literature about goal-setting. We've been told that high achievers are those who are out there enthusiastically setting goals. We hear the most about the importance of SMART goals—those that are specific, measurable, achievable, relevant, and time bound. Better goals lead to better results, they say. And yet, if that were true, the person with the best goals would win the CrossFit Games.

In reality, it's the opposite. People tend to focus disproportionately on results, while neglecting the day-to-day things that will get them there. What's the effort you need to put in in order to achieve that goal? Goals are nothing but the results from which you put forth effort.

That effort, that commitment to the process, is the reason that Katrín is standing before me in the warm-up area, excitedly reliving Climbing Snail as if I didn't just watch her do it. She's talking so fast I can barely keep up. "I took a chance on the last rope climb," she says, grinning. "I was barely holding on, so when I touched the top I was like, *yes!*" I laugh. "It's the best I've ever seen you compete at CrossFit Games," I tell her.

Some of the other women return from the soccer field, and Katrín bounces off to exchange high-fives and hugs with her friends. I turn to O'Keefe. Quietly, so as not to jinx myself, I confide in him what my gut says. "Katrín is going to win again."

CHAPTER 8

CONTROL

★

One can have no smaller or greater
mastery than mastery of oneself.

—LEONARDO DA VINCI

SATURDAY, JULY 23, 2016
STUBHUB CENTER, CARSON, CA

During the Games, the athlete warm-up area is like our office. It's where we spend the most time throughout the day, whether we're getting loose for an event, killing time between briefings, or rendezvousing after heats. It's the same for practically all the other athletes, which makes the warm-up area the social epicenter of the CrossFit Games. For the most part, everyone does their own thing here.

Many of the athletes are friends, but they're all business while competing and tend to keep to themselves. Nevertheless, the athlete area is a constant buzz of trending topics that evolve throughout the week. After the next event is unveiled, the buzz is particularly noisy.

It's not hard to understand why. There is a lot going on in the Separator.

EVENT 9:

THE SEPARATOR (MEN)	THE SEPARATOR (WOMEN)
For Time:	For Time:
12 Ring Handstand Push-Ups	15 Back Squats (165 lb.)
15 Back Squats (225 lb.)	20 Burpees
20 Burpees	6 Ring Handstand Push-Ups
9 Ring Handstand Push-Ups	18 Front Squats (145 lb.)
18 Front Squats (205 lb.)	20 Burpees
20 Burpees	4 Ring Handstand Push-Ups
6 Ring Handstand Push-Ups	21 Overhead Squats (125 lb.)
21 Overhead Squats (185 lb.)	20 Burpees
20 Burpees	2 Ring Handstand Push-Ups

When the athletes return to the warm-up area after their briefing, the buzz erupts almost immediately. Much of the talk centers around the ring handstand push-ups, a movement being tested at the Games for the first time since 2010. But it doesn't end there. The athletes are stressing about the standards for the workout, griping about their heat times, predicting which athletes will perform well, discussing the leaderboard, and debating the impact that the last workout will have on their performance in this one.

I listen to the buzz with growing content. This is the part of the process from which my athletes derive a considerable competitive advantage. As an elite athlete, there are only five things that you can truly control—your training, nutrition, sleep, recovery, and mindset. If it doesn't fall into one of those categories, I tell my athletes, forget about it. Control the things you can control, and ignore everything else.

This concept of control versus concern is the cornerstone of the process, and it is something we reinforce constantly. Before the Games this year, Katrín, Cole, and I spent a month holed up in Cape Cod, training without distractions. One of the first things we did upon arriving was sit down and make a list. I asked them to write down every possible thing they could think of that could go wrong at the CrossFit Games. They took the exercise to heart—the final list had 101 items on it, including things like the weather, alarm clocks not going off, nutritional distress, judges miscounting reps, travel delays, and shark attacks. We named the list "101 Things That Could Go Wrong at the Games," then went through it one by one, categorizing each item into things we could and couldn't control. The things we couldn't control got erased from our minds, and the things we could control got a plan.

A huge piece of chasing excellence is attention to tiny details, but the key distinction is that you pay attention to the *right* details, the ones within your control and over which you have power. Most people go through life having no idea what they can actually control. They're *concerned* about a lot of things, but that doesn't mean they *control* those things. Many people struggle to recognize the difference between the two. Imagine a book of matches. A typical matchbook has twenty matches, and together, they represent all your energy for the day. Energy is a finite resource; once it's gone, you can't get it back. If you burn through your matchsticks on things that are outside your control, you have less energy for things you can control—things that can actually move the needle on your performance.

In the sport of CrossFit, there is so much that lies beyond our control. All the buzz in the athlete area falls into this category. No amount of concern will enable us to control things like the weather, workouts, standards, judges, or other athletes. Whether we're training in December at home or competing at the Games in July, I coach my athletes not to focus on anyone's performance but their own. We don't say, *Look at how much he can lift or how fast she ran. I have to beat that.* They're only competing with themselves.

If I were to tell Mat, "Okay, going into this event, you have to beat these three guys," what action would that translate into? How would he achieve that direction? Take it to a different sport, even. In the NBA, you'll hear coaches during time-outs trying to rally their teams by directing them with comments like, "Okay, we're down by ten. We've got to bring it within five by halftime. Go out there and bring it within five." But what does that direction mean? Obviously, the players want to score as many points as they can, and it's not like they haven't been trying. It's akin to telling them, "Just do better!" *Bring it within five?* There are so many external factors—the calls from the ref, plays from the other team—that keep the score beyond their control. What would work far better is an actionable cue: "Stop forcing outside jumpers; we need to get the ball to our big men in the paint. We can dominate them on the post. And on defense, we are switching to a full court press and challenging the inbound pass." That's something that's within the players' control.

Once you learn to ignore the things you can't control, the next step is to identify the things you can control and should be focusing on. A good way to do this is to start with the end in mind and work backward. What are the performance metrics, habits, and hallmarks of the super-high achievers in your field? If you're a politician, these things might be your constituents, policy knowledge, networking, and public speaking. Once you've identified the things over which you have control, the next step is to take extreme ownership of them. Sticking with the politician example, start with constituent relations. Things you can control might include meeting with constituents two to three times a week, tracking voter opinion, hosting a town hall meeting once a month, and replying professionally and punctually to constituent mail. Being knowledgeable on policy might mean reading two to three newspapers a day, attending briefings, and reading issue-specific books or articles. Networking might include how often you're attending events, how quickly you follow up with new contacts, how often you touch base with existing contacts, and so on. Once you identify the things you can control, success is a matter of maximizing every detail, every day.

For my athletes, there are five things completely within our control—training, nutrition, sleep, recovery, and mindset. Within each area, we have identified five to ten specific daily tasks or habits that are essential to our ability to make progress. Inside the training category, for example, there are specific warm-up and cool-down techniques and a prescribed number of days they will swim each week. Nutrition is comprised of eating a specific quantity of carbohydrates, protein, and fat at certain times as well as pre- and post-training fueling protocols. We dial in their sleep by tracking total hours and the quality of their sleep, as well as creating a nightly routine that promotes more restful nights. We maximize recovery by having the athletes schedule regular sauna sessions, professional body work, muscle stim, and more. The athletes are accountable for the development of their mental toughness through a pre-training mindfulness practice on a daily basis, as well as other character-development exercises.

Every day, week in and week out, these are the things we focus on. Identifying the controllables and owning them in this way takes the mystery out of success. Achievement becomes the result of how committed you are to following the process.

All of this is summed up by the tattoo on Mat's left arm—the Serenity Prayer. You've heard it before:

> God grant me the serenity to accept the things I cannot change, the courage to change the things I can, and the wisdom to know the difference.

It doesn't matter whether you believe in God or not—this is exactly the mantra you want to lean in to. Let go of what you can't change. Make room for the things you can.

* * *

In case anyone thought performing ring handstand push-ups was too straightforward, the rings for the Separator have been hung seven feet in the air, so that the men have to perform a muscle-up in order to get into position. It makes the event far more challenging, but it also makes the standard more difficult to judge. Standing seven feet below the athletes, staring up into the setting sun, the judges are at a challenging angle.

The result is a bit chaotic—after a relatively uneventful

opening round of twelve, Mat returns back to the rings for the round of nine and receives a flurry of no-reps. From where I'm sitting, it's hard to tell why—his shoulders are touching the rings at the bottom, and his elbows are visibly locked out at the top. Mat shakes his head but keeps his cool. He jumps back up on the rings and gets back to work. He gets another no-rep, and then is awarded a good rep on his next attempt, which looks exactly the same.

Getting no-repped is frustrating. In a sport where seconds can, and often do, mean the difference between first place and tenth place, no-reps are costly. And yet, as an athlete, you have no control over the call your judge makes. All you can do is move well; anything else is a waste of time and energy. Mat knows this, but the seemingly arbitrary calls are starting to eat away at his composure. After three more punishing no-reps in a row, he dismounts from the rings and looks almost pleadingly at his judge. He holds up three fingers and shakes his head. Then, as if thinking better of it, he turns and walks behind the rings to collect himself. He takes a deep breath, shakes out his shoulders, and you can actually see the will spread across his face as it is summoned in real time.

Meanwhile, Josh Bridges has pulled ahead. He's cranking through the handstand push-ups faster than Mat and is going to arrive at the final barbell well in front. It's an eerily familiar scene. In the final event of last year's CrossFit Games, Mat was in a similar race with Ben Smith on handstand push-ups. Ben was moving through them faster than Mat, which was bewildering to Mat at the time—Mat is among the best in the world at handstand push-ups, and he knew it. Instead of controlling his own performance, he tried to match Ben's pace. He was, after all, one of the best in the world at handstand push-ups, so of course he should be able to keep up with Ben. But playing your game while adjusting for someone else's is like trying to inhale and exhale at the same time—it's impossible. Ultimately, it cost Mat the title.

But this isn't 2015, and the Mat Fraser on the floor now is not the same athlete he was a year ago. Instead of looking around and gauging his position relative to the other competitors, he's focused solely on that which is within his control—what he's capable of *right now*, in this minute. As Josh finishes his handstand push-ups and moves on to the barbell, Mat looks unperturbed. He doesn't look around; he doesn't try to speed up. He simply jumps back up on the rings and continues working.

By the time Mat finishes his handstand push-ups, Josh is working on his overhead squats. Josh isn't known for his strength, but he's a fierce competitor and is feeding off the adrenaline of the electric crowd. When Mat arrives at the barbell, the StubHub Center seems to stand as one as the former Junior National Weightlifting Champion gets his barbell overhead and starts eating into Josh's lead. When Mat draws even with him, the crowd loses its mind—I've never heard the tennis stadium so loud. Inspired by their raucous encouragement, Mat advances his barbell without putting it down and pulls ahead of Josh for the first time in the workout. He polishes off the final set of overhead squats, then sprints to the finish and takes the heat win, putting an exclamation point on his mental metamorphosis.

The crowd is still on its feet, and I join them in their enthusiastic applause. Mat has been putting on a show all week long, but I'm most proud of this performance. It's easy to compete with excellence when things are going your way; maintaining your composure when everything seems to be working against you is far more impressive, and it's something we've worked hard on over the last year.

After his heat, Mat is wrangled by a sideline reporter for an interview. The reporter notes that the final event of the day still hasn't been released, and asks Mat what he thinks Dave Castro has in store for tonight. Mat looks annoyed. The words aren't even out of the reporter's mouth and Mat is frowning and shaking his head. "I don't guess events," he says. "Waste of time."

Control what you can control. Ignore everything else.

CHAPTER 9

TURN THE PAGE

★

You will become clever through your mistakes.
—GERMAN PROVERB

SATURDAY, JULY 23, 2016
STUBHUB CENTER, CARSON, CA

The final event on Saturday is unveiled thirty minutes after the last heat of the Separator. It will be the shortest event yet—a barn-burner sprint of box jumps and D-Ball cleans. "It's one of those workouts where you just have to set yourself on fire," observes Pat Sherwood cheerfully. "The pace is *GO*."

EVENT 10:
100 Percent

For Time:
40 Box Jumps (men 30″/women 24″)
20 D-Ball Cleans (men 150 lb. / women 100 lb.)

Less than an hour after leaving it, the women jog back down the steps of the tennis stadium for the final event of the day. Thanks to a second-place finish in the Separator, Katrín is wearing the leader jersey for the first time all weekend. Though she has now beaten Tia in three consecutive events, she leads by only twelve points. To the announcers and the fans, it's starting to feel like a championship-prize fight between the two women, and this event is going to be an important round.

At the sound of the starting beep, the women race toward the line of plyo boxes and begin bounding over them. After forty reps, there is literally no separation—all twenty women finish their box jumps at the exact same time. As they advance to the D-Balls, the race is so close that it's impossible to tell who's ahead. The pace is blindingly fast—there's no room for mistakes.

Katrín makes a big one.

A D-Ball is nothing more than a rubber ball, slightly larger than a basketball, filled with sand. Cleaning it is decidedly more unwieldy than cleaning a barbell—you have to scoop it off the ground using your hands and forearms, hoist it into your lap, and then explosively jump it up over your shoulders. The twenty D-Ball cleans for this event are completed in two different stations—after the first ten cleans, the athletes advance their ball forward, then complete the final ten reps.

One of the standards for the D-Ball clean is that every rep must be finished over the shoulder, behind the athlete. Katrín advances her ball forward and drops it in front of her. *No rep.* She continues working, unfazed, but the damage is done. As fast as it started, the event is over. All at once, six women drop their D-Ball and sprint, dive, and slide over the finish mat. Katrín, as I suspected, is half a step behind them. She streaks across the line seconds after Tia and Sara. I glance up at the jumbotron, which announces the final placements and times. Six seconds separate first place from ninth place, and two seconds is the difference between third place and eighth. Katrín has finished seventh—the two seconds she lost to her D-Ball no-rep cost her at least four places. Down on the finish mat, she returns the hugs of the other competitors and maintains her composure, but I can tell by her body language that she's furious at herself.

I head back to the athlete area, where I know Katrín will be waiting for me. The men are already in the staging area behind the stadium, so the warm-up area is pitch dark and deserted. I find her standing next to a row of abandoned plyo boxes. She looks crestfallen.

"A stupid mistake," she spits. "Accept it," I tell her. "Let it sit for another five minutes, then we'll move on." She nods wordlessly, trying to hold back tears, and sits down on one of the boxes. She stares at the pavement for a few minutes, shoulders slumped. To the outside observer, it would be easy to assume Katrín is despondent because she took seventh place and lost the overall lead. But that doesn't check out—just earlier today, she deemed a sixth-place finish in Climbing Snail "the happiest I've ever been." How can one placement produce such a drastically different set of emotions?

Because the leaderboard has nothing to do with it. Katrín goes into the CrossFit Games with one goal: at the end of the week, she wants to be able to look herself in the eye and have no regrets. Regardless of where she ends up on the leaderboard, she'll walk away happy if she knows she was able to give everything she had, every minute of every event. Katrín is upset because she knows that performance was not her best effort. She made an easily avoidable mistake in an event with no room for error, and gave up valuable points in the process. That mistake was a regret, one that might haunt her when the points are totaled at the end of the weekend.

Is it unfortunate? Yes. But when you're going that fast and giving it all you've got, you're going to make mistakes. No basketball team plays an entire game without fouls; no tennis player plays three sets without finding the net. I can deal with mistakes. What I can't deal with is a lapse in effort—and Katrín certainly didn't have a lack of effort.

"All we do now is turn the page," I tell her. "What can you do right now, in this moment, to prep yourself for tomorrow? Anything we do looking back doesn't help that. Now we look forward."

The way we do that in our sport, where we have multiple events in one day, is with a specific protocol. With the quick turnover time between events, we don't have the luxury of grieving or celebrating for extended periods of time, and we certainly can't sit there and analyze things— there's just no time. After every workout, we debrief for five to ten minutes. If the event went great, we have a quick high-five celebration. If it's a bad event, we have a short grieving session. Both are part of the process, but then you need to be able to turn the page. If you don't allow for that—if you don't let yourself grieve for five minutes—it'll haunt you; you won't be able to shake it off.

It's important to be able to turn the page after a bad event. Staying in a negative mindset will undermine confidence, without which Katrín—or anyone else for that matter—cannot hope to compete with excellence. With the point spread so tight between the leaders, her mindset is going to be a deciding factor tomorrow, on the final day of competition. To defend her title, Katrín needs to hit the reset button and start anew in the morning as though this event never happened.

It's easier said than done. After a bad performance, it's natural to feel frustrated and emotional. It's easy to say you're turning the page, but it's much harder to control the negative thoughts that want to drift back into your mind. Like everything else, it's a skill—one that we practice every day. The first thing my athletes do when they get to the gym in the morning—before they warm up, mobilize, or touch a barbell—is lie on the floor with their legs up and their eyes closed and practice breathing for ten minutes. The goal of these breathing exercises is multifaceted. On the physiological side, we're trying to get better oxygen exchange, improve lung capacity, and learn more efficient, diaphragmatic breathing. But the psychological aspect is just as important and has less to do with breathing than mindfulness.

Mindfulness is the study of your own mind, and how to train your mind. Properly executed, it is the basic human ability to be fully present, aware of where we are and what we're doing, and not overly reactive or overwhelmed by what's going on around us. The goal of our breathing exercises is to live in the present moment with nonjudgment, open-mindedness, and positivity. Can you focus on your breath and only your breath for ten straight minutes? The answer is no, you can't. So, when you can't, what is your mind doing? Are you reflecting on the past—*I can't believe I lost my train of thought, I'm so bad at this*, and so on—or are you focusing on the present moment, trying to reclaim your train of thought without judging yourself? If you can stay present in a controlled environment, that transfers over to when you have a bad event. This exercise in mindfulness is a microcosm of what will happen in the real world when you'll want to lay judgment on yourself, when you'll abandon the present moment and struggle to stay positive. We practice every single day so, when these moments arise, we know how to move forward productively.

From time to time, we also get the chance to practice this in training. A month before the Games, when Katrín, Cole, and I were training on Cape Cod, we were at Upper Cape CrossFit, working through a dense volume day. One of the many workouts we did that day was a couplet of muscle-ups and overhead squats. It's one of the best combinations possible for Cole, and he breezed through it. Katrín, who struggles with muscle-ups, did not. Struggle is not a bad thing at all; in fact, it's a great thing—struggle makes you better. The problem was that she mentally checked out. About halfway through the workout she got frustrated. Instead of embracing the struggle, she took her foot off the gas pedal and just coasted half-heartedly through the rest of the workout. She had reverted, temporarily, to the immature and emotional athlete we'd spent the last two years vanquishing.

When Katrín finished her last muscle-up, she beelined straight for the door and shut it behind her. I followed her out there. She didn't want to talk; she was very reluctant to do anything except wallow in her own pity. I talked her through why moments like this are important. "We're going to have moments like this at the Games," I told her. "We're going to have events that feel like this. We're going to be frustrated. We're never going to have fifteen events in a row of sunshine and rainbows—it's just not going to happen. We're going to be frustrated at least once, if not multiple times, during Games week. When that happens, are we going to give up and host a pity party? Are we going to let it linger? Are we going to live in that moment for longer than we need to?"

"This is exactly what it's going to feel like," I told her. "Let's use this moment, right now, to learn how to turn the page. We need to learn how to take advantage of the next available moments, which are not affected whatsoever by what just happened. It's gone. Once it's happened, it no longer exists. Particularly in a sport like ours, where every event is completely different and has absolutely no bearing on the next one, living in the past is a liability that will diminish future opportunities."

By focusing on that lesson, we were able to turn what could have been the worst training day of the year into the best one of the year. If you were to ask Katrín what her best training day of 2016 was, I know, without a doubt, she'd point to that day at the Cape.

Understanding that you only have control over the present moment is the key to being able to turn the page. Reliving the past is a recipe for unnecessary depression, and fearing the future is a surefire way to anxiety. Learning to live in the present moment is vital, because it's the only thing you have any control over. The only thing you can do to rectify the past or influence the future is to take action *now*, in the present moment.

It's a difficult skill to master. It's not the kind of thing you can just wave off and hope that it'll be there on game day. It takes practice. The discipline with which Katrín practices mindfulness has made it automatic. We spend time learning how to turn the page in training so she can do it when it matters. Her daily breathing and that day on the Cape prepared her for this moment, where her ability to reclaim her positivity and move forward will be a competitive advantage tomorrow, on the final day of competition. The importance of this cannot be over-stated. With the competition so close, these are the things that matter. When physical abilities are equal, mindset becomes the separator.

Katrín is quiet as we walk through the dark, empty parking lot to the car. We walk in silence for a few minutes, and then she glances over at me, a slow smile spreading across her face. "How cool is it that I have the opportunity to come from behind tomorrow?"

CHAPTER 10

HUMILITY

★

Winning takes talent. To repeat it takes character.
—JOHN WOODEN

SATURDAY, JULY 23, 2016
STUBHUB CENTER, CARSON, CA

Off-limits to spectators, one floor below the mezzanine, the underbelly of the StubHub Center is a teeming hive of CrossFit Games support staff. Red-shirted medical personnel bandage scrapes and tape ankles. Black-shirted photographers swap out lenses and replace batteries. Yellow-shirted scoring staff consult stacks of scorecards and one another. Navy-shirted judges down bottles of water between heats. Gray-shirted equipment teams load barbells, stack bumper plates, and drag rowers in every direction.

It's also where blue-shirted Athlete Control staff corral the competitors before their heats. They stand under the only decoration, a quote painted on the wall of the tunnel connecting the soccer and tennis stadiums: "Sports do not build character, they reveal it." It's a fitting reminder on the last day of competition. With the points race on the women's side so close, character, as much as physical ability, will decide who stands on the top of the podium at the end of the day.

The first three events of the day will happen back-to-back-to-back on the soccer field. There is virtually no rest between them—once the athletes take the field, they'll remain in their lane for a brief reset period before the start of the next event.

EVENT 11:	EVENT 12:	EVENT 13:
Handstand Walk	Suicide Sprint	The Plow
For Time:	For Time:	For Time:
280' Handstand Walk	840' Shuttle Sprint	560' Plow Drag

The handstand walk is up first. Katrín strides out of the tunnel, eyes narrowed, and I know it will be a cold day in hell before she loses this event. Katrín, a former elite gymnast, is the best CrossFit athlete in the world at handstand walks; when it comes to walking on her hands, she's in a class by herself. Her strategy is straightforward—kick up, walk to the finish line, and don't come down until you're there. She's the only woman to walk the entire 280 feet without coming down once. She takes the event win, her second of the week, then collects herself for the start of Suicide Sprint.

The shuttle sprint takes place on the same 280-foot course as the handstand walk. The athletes sprint a third of the way down and back, then two-thirds of the way down and back, then sprint the full length of the field to the finish line. Katrín, who is a decent, but not exceptional sprinter, takes tenth.

As the competitors catch their breath, the equipment team emerges from the tunnel like oxen, dragging yet another new implement onto the field. The Plow is exactly what it sounds like—a clunky, weighted metal frame with handles. Event 13 is uncontrived grunt work: drag the Plow down to the end of the field, then turn around and drag it back— as fast as possible. It's something Katrín has never been good at, but we've spent much of the last year improving her ability to move odd objects from one place to another.

As the women take to the starting mats for the final time, I'm expecting Katrín to do well.

I'm wrong.

She *annihilates* it.

She takes off like a sled dog and never lets up; most of the women are walking, but Katrín is somehow jogging. She crosses the finish line in first place, staggers a few steps on shaky legs, then collapses into the grass. She hauls herself up a few minutes later and limps off the field with the help of some of the event staff. The crowd murmurs worriedly around me, but I'm not concerned—Kat isn't injured, she just left absolutely everything she had out on the field. This is what full effort looks like.

The men are up next.

Mat raises eyebrows by taking second in the handstand walk, but the sprint event is what everyone is waiting to watch. Last year at the Games, there were two sprint events, and Mat finished close to last in both of them. As the course is reset and the men line back up to begin Event 12, everyone is expecting a similar outcome—finally, an event that Mat Fraser will finish in the middle of the pack.

From the moment the starting beep blares, it is obvious that everyone is wrong. Mat and Ben Smith leap out to an early lead. Ben is quicker around the pylons, but Mat is catching him on the straightaways. As they round the final pylon, Ben is a few meters ahead. Then they hit the final stretch, and Mat looks as though he's taken a shot of adrenaline to the heart. He's still trailing Ben, but he's closing like a freight train; by the time they reach midfield, Mat has narrowed the margin to a single stride. With 50 feet to go, Mat draws even, and the crowd lets out a roar so loud I'm fairly sure I'll never hear normally again. Ben looks over at Mat at the moment he passes him with an expression that says, *This wasn't the plan. You're not supposed to be doing this.* Mat passes Ben 30 feet before the finish and storms across the line to win his heat. "What can't this guy do?!" shouts commentator Sean Woodland over the mic.

As Mat crosses the finish line, he pumps both fists together and gives one of the barricades a celebratory shake. His demons from the 2015 sprints thoroughly exorcised, he looks fired up for the first time all week. It's the proudest he's been of himself all weekend, and with good reason. After last year's Games, when he won silver for the second year in a row, he looked inwardly without ego and knew he had to improve his running. So, he did what few athletes would have the humility to do—he reached out to the local high school track coach and asked if he could practice with the team a few nights a week. Then he got his ass handed to him two nights a week for six months.

"Everything you're supposed to be doing during sprinting, I was doing the exact opposite," Mat told me. "My technique was *terrible*."

Sprinting with the Essex high school track team was incredibly humbling for Mat. He went from an environment where he was comfortable and dominant—CrossFit—to getting thrashed by ninth and tenth graders. Imagine the awkwardness of a stocky, bearded, tattooed, mid-twenties guy toeing the line with lanky teenagers and getting smoked in every drill and sprint. Mat didn't care. He wanted to get better, and this would make him better.

It's a character trait that Mat and Katrín have in common. It's hard to tell from her dominant performance in the Plow, but she used to be terrible at odd-object work. The first time this was really exposed was during the 2015 Games training on the Cape. We had a handful of athletes down there, and we were doing some sled work with an *extremely* heavy sled. The distance was short—50 feet down, 50 feet back. The other women in the group slogged it out—they pushed the sled down and back, then crumpled to the ground, completely spent. Katrín, however, couldn't get the sled to move a single foot. No matter how hard she tried, she was physically unable to move it *at all*. When it came to odd objects, she couldn't hide behind any of her strengths—her world-class engine was useless, her finely honed gymnastics skills irrelevant, and she couldn't technique her way around it. Moving heavy loads from one place to another comes down to raw, brute-force horsepower, and she had almost none. It was by far the biggest hole in her game.

Realizing how limiting that was, we put it into her training every day. After she won the Games that year, every training day had some move-it-from-here-to-there component, and Fridays were reserved exclusively for odd-object work. We practiced moving logs, carrying stones, flipping tires, and walking yokes—everything she wasn't good at.

It takes an uncommon amount of humility for anyone to submit themselves to doing things they're bad at every single day. It's just not a good time. It's even harder to do when you're at the top of your chosen endeavor, as Mat and Katrín are. When you're the best in the world at something, everyone is watching you. Expectations are high—you're expected to be sensational at everything, all the time. It's an unrealistic standard, to be sure, but one that exists anyway. It takes extraordinary humility to continue to work your weaknesses at this level, because it's an admission that you're not the best, or even very good, at some things. People don't expect champions to struggle or fail. Some people will look at you and scoff. They'll talk. When you reach a certain level, it's far easier to hide in your strengths because of the ego-boost they provide—you feel good, you look good, and people are in awe. But it's a trap; the moment you believe you've arrived at the door of greatness, it will be slammed in your face.

Humility is an essential component of success. People like Mat and Katrín, who can look in the mirror and identify their weaknesses, are the people who grow the most. Business theorist Chris Argyris, in his book *Teaching Smart People How to Learn*, outlines why constant self-evaluation is the key to personal advancement:

> Most people define learning too narrowly as mere "problem-solving," so they focus on identifying and correcting errors in the external environment. Solving problems is important. But if learning is to persist, they must also look inward. They need to reflect critically on their own behavior, identify the ways they often inadvertently contribute to the organization's problems, and then change how they act.

Argyris used these insights to come up with the idea of "double-loop learning." Single-loop learners search for external factors to explain why they're not succeeding; they put it down as having the wrong coach, the wrong program, the wrong equipment, the wrong people around them, or what have you. Double-loop learners iterate, and then look inward for the solutions to problems that arise. They're the kind of people who can take a hard look in the mirror and tell their reflection, "I'm the reason I'm not succeeding," and then proactively change into a better version of themselves. They figure out their weaknesses, fix them, test, and then reevaluate; in the cycle, there is always a deep look inward built in.

It's easy to distinguish between different learners in personal and professional relationships. Single-loop learners look to their spouses, partners, bosses, or subordinates for reasons why things aren't going well; they blame everything on other people. There's always a reason why problems can be traced back to the other person in the relationship. Double-loop learners, however, take ownership of problems; they think: *There must be something I'm doing that's making my spouse/partner/coworker react this way.* They take complete ownership of their situations. They dig deep to figure out where the disconnect is and where they can improve. They shoulder blame *and* find solutions.

In the long run, double-loop learners are much more successful than single-loop learners. People who have the capacity to own their problems are the ones who will most quickly discover solutions to those problems.

Martina Navratilova, the legendary tennis player, had a

uniquely long career; she enjoyed a long peak and played into her forties. When she found herself on the downswing of her career, she knew she'd need to reinvent herself and her game to have a shot at continuing to play. So, she did exactly that: she started strength training, worked on new aspects of her game, improved her nutrition, and improved the team around her. She continued to have one of the longest and most successful tennis careers of all time. Navratilova had the grit to know it was up to her to keep making progress, that talent alone wouldn't get her to the next level.

If it seems as if my team spends an inordinate amount of time focusing on character, it's because we do. The most battle-tested, unimpeachable process is nothing unless it is accompanied by the character traits needed to make it stick. Humility is a huge part of the equation; it's one of the cornerstones of the process—the only way I can make my team better is by acknowledging their limitations. They're not the best in the world at everything, not even close. As a coach, it's my job to continually look for weaknesses—for areas where we can be beat. The second I feel as if Katrín, Mat, or Cole can't be beat, we've failed.

The talk among the commentators and fans this morning is a reminder of how easy it can be to fall victim to complacency. It seems as if all anyone is talking about on the final day of competition is Mat's dominant performance. "Sunday is turning into a victory lap for Mat Fraser," says one of the commentators, and it's a sentiment shared by practically everyone in the StubHub Center. Mat walking through the complex is like Moses parting the Red Sea—fans stop him every 30 feet to ask for a selfie or congratulate him, as though he's already won. The math is convincing, but nothing is over until it's over, and there are still two events to go.

CHAPTER 11

COMPETITIVE EXCELLENCE

★

*Excellence is the gradual result of
always wanting to do better.*

—PAT RILEY

SUNDAY, JULY 24, 2016
STUBHUB CENTER, CARSON, CA

After the field events, the athletes are swept straight from
the soccer complex to the tennis court to be briefed on the
next event. All eighty competitors file through the tunnel
that connects the two structures. Everyone is moving

slowly—their quads, hamstrings, and lower backs are lit up—and most are still covered in grass after collapsing to the ground after the Plow. The tennis court is close to 100 degrees; the athletes gather around Dave wearing hats, bags of ice, or T-shirts on their heads.

The next event is cardio purgatory.

EVENT 14:
Rope Chipper

For Time:
200 m Ski Erg
50/40 Double-Unders
200 m Row
50/40 Double-Unders
0.4-mile Assault Air Bike
50/40 Double-Unders
200 m Row
50/40 Double-Unders
200 m Ski Erg
90-ft. Sled Pull (men 310 lb. / women 220 lb.)

I meet up with Mat and Katrín as they exit the stadium after the briefing. As we walk back to the warm-up area, they confer about the workout. "I think you're going to be able to go faster than you think you can," Mat tells

Katrín. "It's ski erg, rower, bike," he says. "We live on that shit." They grin at each other conspiratorially. "And the sled pull is whatever," Mat says. "Just get that pump for the finish line," he jokes.

Now back in the warm-up area, Mat starts getting loose on the rower. He's wearing the same outfit he's been wearing since Day 2 of the competition—the white leader jersey and corresponding red shorts. At this point, they smell pretty bad. Reebok, the title sponsor of the Cross-Fit Games and official gear provider, was obviously not prepared for the same person to lead the entire week. Mat was issued his customized leader jersey on Wednesday and has been competing in it ever since. When O'Keefe asked why Mat could only be issued one jersey, a Reebok representative shrugged sheepishly. "We've never had this issue before."

Add it to the list of records Mat has collected throughout the week. He has more top-ten finishes than any other competitor in Games history and, with two events to go, the largest lead in Games history. As he jogs down the stairs of the tennis stadium, he is 195 points ahead of second-place-ranked Ben Smith. Though Rope Chipper is not the final event of competition, Mat can seal his victory as the Fittest Man on Earth in this event as long as he doesn't come in last place.

The men fan out and line up on their starting mats. Mat immediately rips off his pungent shirt. O'Keefe, sitting beside me, laughs. Good thing they also have leader shorts. The starting beep echoes through the tennis stadium, and Rope Chipper is underway. The men storm through the ski erg and arrive at the double-unders at the same time. These are far from standard-issue jump ropes—the handles weigh a pound each, and the cables are weighted—but it's impossible to tell; all the competitors make it look far easier than it should.

Mat finishes his first set of fifty, or at least he thinks he does, and puts his rope down. His judge, however, signals that he's not done. I can practically hear Mat roll his eyes, but he picks up his rope and does one more rep, then sprints to the Assault Bike to join the rest of the pack. He's the first one off the bike and advances to the second round of double-unders. He has the same miscommunication with his judge again—once again, he stops as if finished, then has to complete one more rep.

By the time Mat gets off the rower, he's in the middle of the pack; as he advances to the final round of double-unders, half the field is five to seven seconds ahead of him. There is no miscommunication this time—he does his last fifty reps in two sets of twenty-five, then races after the leaders, who are already on the last ski erg. The final element of the workout is a 90-foot sled pull. Mat is still trailing the handful of leaders, but it couldn't matter less; in less than a minute, he will win the CrossFit Games. But here he is, dragging his 310-pound sled like his life depends on it. He's the fifth man in his heat to yank his sled across the line, good enough for tenth overall. When he steps on his finish mat, he has, by virtue of math, won the 2016 CrossFit Games.

Mat's attitude on the floor, victory all but assured, is the pinnacle of competitive excellence: *I will maximize my minutes by thinking, acting, training, and competing with excellence, regardless of circumstances.* Mat had already won (he was never going to finish last in Rope Chipper) but didn't let the scoreboard influence his performance. He competed as though Ben Smith was twenty points behind him, not two hundred.

As if to illustrate this point, he comes storming out of the tennis stadium after the event. He strides up to me and O'Keefe, shaking his head. "The guy was counting out loud and saying fifty!" Mat says, throwing his hands in the air. "He was counting a rep ahead, so I was stopping because he said 'fifty,' and I thought I was done!" It takes both me and O'Keefe a second to realize what he's so fired up about—the miscommunication with his judge during the double-unders. O'Keefe asks what the head judge said when he came over. "He came over and said my rep count was correct," Mat says, rolling his eyes. "I know it's correct! But the judge keeps saying 'fifty' too early!"

As we walk, I try to hide my smile. Mat has been trying to win the CrossFit Games for three years. And now, with his victory a mathematical certainty, he's pissed off because he didn't win by a larger margin. It reminds me of the 2012 college football national championship, when Alabama trounced Notre Dame in a 42–14 beatdown.

With just more than seven minutes remaining in the fourth quarter, with Alabama holding a commanding lead, quarterback AJ McCarron and center Barrett Jones got their pre-snap signals crossed. As a result, Alabama earned a delay-of-game penalty. McCarron and Jones exchanged heated words, and then something strange happened: the center forcefully shoved the quarterback.

To almost everyone watching, the scene was perplexing. Alabama was up twenty-eight points, facing a meaningless second-and-six with a national title all but assured; practically any other team would have been celebrating. But premature celebrating is simply not what Alabama players do. They are disciples of Coach Nick Saban's process, and the process is about doing your job to the best of your ability, right now, regardless of circumstance.

McCarron and Jones were so detached from results and so committed to performing at their maximum potential that they got into a shoving match on national TV.

Alabama coach Nick Saban loved it, for all the same reasons I love Mat's attitude during Rope Chipper. Mat has already won the CrossFit Games, and he's still out on the floor hustling after every point. He doesn't care that he has a 195-point lead with only two events left—he's still out there trying to be the best.

If you can compete with excellence when you're way ahead, you can do it when you're way behind. Like everything else, excellence is a habit.

There might be no greater example of this than the New England Patriots, who overcame the largest deficit in Super Bowl history to beat the Atlanta Falcons and clinch the title in 2017. At the end of the third quarter, they trailed 28–3. Instead of wallowing in premature defeat, the Patriot players on the sidelines were doing the opposite—telling each other what a great story this was going to be. Film from the game shows Tom Brady marching up and down the sideline, exhorting his teammates: "Let's go! Let's show some fight! Let's play harder! Harder! Tougher! Everything!" Think about how unusual that is. With only seventeen minutes left to play, the Patriots were down by *twenty-five points* against the best offense in the league. It was an insurmountable margin; no team in history had ever come back from more than a ten-point deficit to win a Super Bowl. But neither Brady nor any of the other Patriot players ever considered themselves out of the game.

New England wasn't concerned with the scoreboard, because they were committed to the process. Instead of focusing on the scale of their task, they focused on making one play, then making another. After mustering only a field goal on their first seven drives, they scored on their final five possessions. Patriots wide receiver Julian Edelman said it best after the game: "It's the microcosm of our life, our season. Mental toughness, believe, do your job, work hard, and we'll be champions in the championship game."

Nick Saban's Crimson Tide and Bill Belichick's Patriots are two of the best examples of competitive excellence I can think of. I tell these stories and show video clips to my CrossFit Games athletes, as well as athletes that attend training camps at my gym, to reinforce what competitive excellence looks like in practice—unwavering commitment to the process, regardless of what's going on around you.

Competitive excellence is not a switch you can just flip on game day. You can't train on autopilot and compete with purpose. In order to perform at the highest level in competition, you have to prepare that way every single day. When Mat goes to the gym, he doesn't show up just to get the programmed training in. He comes to *compete*. He trains like he's *possessed*. The gym is where and when he builds his competitive edge, and you can see the result of that mindset every time he takes the floor in competition. Mat is able to compete with excellence because he trains with excellence, day in and day out.

The principle of competitive excellence applies to everyone, not just CrossFit Games athletes. Regardless of your chosen profession, being the best means taking advantage of every opportunity that each day brings. Success is not achieved by an occasional heroic response, but with focused and sustained action. Excellence can only be achieved today—not yesterday or tomorrow—because they don't exist in the present moment. It's the not-so-hidden secret to extraordinary success: clarify what you really want, then work as hard as you can for as long as it takes.

.

CHAPTER 12

CLUTCH

★

In any game played with the body,
it's the head that counts.

—JAMES KERR

SUNDAY, JULY 24, 2016
STUBHUB CENTER, CARSON, CA

After five grueling days, it's Sunday afternoon in Carson. The week we've spent the last year training for is over as fast as it started. It happens every year—everyone goes into the CrossFit Games with a kind of Hell Week mentality, mentally prepared to endure the longest, most challenging week of their lives. It ends up being the opposite: You have a couple of events, and then the first day is gone. Right away you're into the next day, which is usually just one event, and then that day is gone. Then all of a sudden it's the weekend. Once Friday is over, you only have two more days of the CrossFit Games. The next thing you know, it's Saturday night. The week unfolds so fast, it feels like time travel.

To the extent possible, I try to prepare my athletes for how fast time flies in competition. I tell them that it's going to be over in a flash, with the hope that they'll take the time to appreciate moments along the way. Like a parent sending kids off to college, I implore them to cherish every single moment and make memories. It doesn't stop the competition from flying by, but they enjoy it more.

Katrín, Mat, and Cole have only one more chance to make the most of it. The final event of the 2016 CrossFit Games is called "Redemption."

EVENT 15:
Redemption
3 Pegboard Ascents
21 Thrusters (men 135 lb. / women 85 lb.)
2 Pegboard Ascents
15 Thrusters (men 135 lb. / women 85 lb.)
1 Pegboard Ascent
9 Thrusters (men 135 lb. / women 85 lb.)

We all knew it was coming—the return of the pegboard. Last year, when the pegboard was introduced at the CrossFit Games for the first time, it stopped the majority of the field in its tracks. Most of the athletes had never seen one before, much less climbed one. The pegboard was part one of a two-part final event in 2015, during which the majority of the women, after failing multiple attempts to climb it, opted to stop and save their energy for part two. It was a strange sight (and not very compelling television), watching the world's fittest women stand helplessly on the competition floor. The men fared slightly better, but still looked out of their element.

But the CrossFit Games are designed to test the athletes, not showcase them. The Games have been exposing weaknesses in the competitors' training in this manner for ten years, constantly pushing the athletes to new heights of physical and mental ability. After the 2015 Games, every athlete went home and bought a pegboard. They've been training on them for a full year and won't be stumped by them again.

In Athlete Village, the competitors warm up for the final time of the 2016 CrossFit Games. The men gather around the lone pegboard in the warm-up area and take turns climbing it. While he waits, Josh Bridges playfully trash-talks Mat. "This guy thinks just because he has a two-hundred-point lead he can walk around here all cockstrong," he says, cracking himself up. "I think Ben's gonna take you, dude," he tells Mat. Josh asks Ben Smith, who's leaning on a nearby GHD, what their point spread is. "Like six hundred," Ben says, playing along. "Oh, you got him!" laughs Josh.

The results on the men's side may be a forgone conclusion, but the women's competition is perilously close. With one event remaining, Katrín leads Tia-Clair Toomey by only twenty-three points. In almost any other event, twenty-three points would be a comfortable cushion, but in this event, it's anything but. Katrín struggles mightily with the pegboard; climbing a pegboard is as hard for her as legless rope climbs used to be. During last year's pegboard event, she was unable to complete a single ascent. So, we went home and practiced. Over the last year, Katrín has trained on the pegboard relentlessly while continuing to build her upper-body pulling strength in general. Despite this, the most she's ever been able to do is *one*.

And so, with the CrossFit Games title on the line, Katrín now faces her biggest weakness. It's a staggering amount of pressure—if Tia finishes in the top three and Katrín finishes outside the top ten, Tia will win the CrossFit Games.

Moments like this are what we train for year-round. It's

why we spend so much time developing character traits like commitment, grit, optimism, and humility. It's the reason we practice embracing adversity and learning to regard it as a competitive advantage. Events like this are the reason behind our all-consuming focus on the process—why we learn to control the things we can and let the rest go.

Katrín and I talk strategy while she warms up on the pegboard. Everything is going to come down to how many pegboards she can make, so it becomes our strategic focus. "There's no reason for you to come out really hot," I tell her. "It's you versus the pegboard, not you versus the other competitors. Be smart. Be mature. No wasted effort. Live in your bubble—don't be influenced by the other women." Kat nods. She knows. I give her one last hug before she goes to check in with Athlete Control, and then we both make our way to the tennis stadium one last time.

The top-ranked women gather at the top of the stadium stairs, announcing the start of the final heat, Redemption. If Katrín is nervous, it's impossible to tell—when her name is announced, she waves both hands over her head and flashes a 56-inch smile. The athletes jog down to the floor, collect their pegs, and then stand in front of the long row of clear Plexiglas pegboards. The starting beep blares, and the last event of the CrossFit Games is underway.

Katrín looks composed and relaxed as she jumps on her pegboard and starts working her way to the top. She makes one, then another, doubling her lifetime total of completed pegboards. She dismounts from the thick red crash mat and stands on the tennis court floor, shaking out her arms. Tia, who is in the lane right next to her, is already on her third ascent. Katrín seems unconcerned; she waits for another twenty seconds, then jumps back up for her third ascent. Halfway up, her biceps give out. Unable to bend her arms, she's dangling by her pegs, arms fully extended. I wince, but she keeps a cool head and does the only thing she's able to do—shimmy up, one peg hole at a time. It's slow going, but she's making it work. She gets to the top, and I watch, heart in my throat, as she starts making her way down. When her feet hit the mat, I realize I've been holding my breath.

Her first round of pegboards completed, Katrín heads to the barbell and gets to work on the thrusters. All the leaders, including Tia, are already back on the pegboard. Kat seems unaware of everything going on around her—she's pacing the barbell work, still being smart. She finishes her set of twenty-one, rolls her barbell forward, and then turns back to the pegboard. She's starting to look spent—her walk back to the pegboard is slow, and she stops in front of the mats to shake out her arms again. Tia, meanwhile, is moving up and down the pegboard like a koala; by the time Katrín arrives to begin her second round, Tia's already done.

These are the moments when it is extremely difficult to stay focused on your own effort. If Katrín takes a quick peek over at Tia and has the thought process of *I have to keep up with her*, if she tries to go up a little too quick and doesn't take the rest she needs, or if she fails just one of those pegboards—she's done.

But Katrín thrives in moments like this. She takes a long break before starting her next ascent, her face a mask of focused composure. Standing in front of her crash mat, she swings her arms back and forth, like a swimmer about to dive in the pool. All around her, the pegboard is starting to take its toll on the other competitors. Sara Sigmundsdóttir, who has been in front of Katrín the entire event, suddenly slips off the pegboard near the top and has to traverse to the other end of the competition floor to retrieve a new set of pegs. When she comes back, Katrín is still staring up at her pegboard.

The crowd is beside itself, urging her back up, but she doesn't seem to notice. Sara begins another attempt, but fails halfway up. Finally, Katrín steps up onto her crash mat, puts her pegs in the bottom holes, and gets started on her fourth ascent. She's still unable to bend her arms at all and is forced to climb the entire way up one hole at a time, on sheer force of will. She lands neatly at the bottom, shakes out her arms, and then, with only two minutes remaining in the event, jumps back up for her fifth ascent. Her arms are completely spent—she has no pulling strength left at all—but she doesn't panic, just methodically shimmies up one hole at a time. I have no idea how she's doing it—this is five times more ascents than her personal best—but she successfully completes the second round and advances back to her barbell.

With only ninety seconds remaining on the clock, Katrín starts to push the pace slightly. She finishes her thrusters unbroken and heads back to the pegboard for the final time. Meanwhile, Tia finishes the event and takes eighth place. Kat is halfway up her last pegboard when time runs out—the event has a ten-minute time cap.

The CrossFit Games are over, but the final result is unclear. There were three other heats of women prior to Katrín's, so it's impossible to know where she finished. Did Tia finish high enough to overtake Katrín? O'Keefe doesn't think so, but there's no way of knowing for sure. All we can do now is wait while the results are tabulated. The women sit anxiously on the mats below the pegboards. The crowd buzzes with apprehension. Three minutes pass, then five, then seven. This seems to be taking an eternity. I look down at Katrín. She hasn't moved in five minutes—she's just sitting on a mat, staring at the floor. My butterflies are flying in tight formation, but my anxiety pales compared to that of my wife, Heather, who is making small squeaking noises, like air being slowly let out of a balloon.

Ten years or ten minutes later, Dave Castro takes the floor, microphone in hand. "Ladies and gentlemen," he begins, "your 2016 Reebok CrossFit Games champion is..." He pauses dramatically, letting his echo bounce around the hushed stadium. His next words are like oxygen. "Once again..." he starts, and the crowd is so apoplectic that they almost drown him out when he announces, "Katrín Davíðsdóttir!"

* * *

Not all of us are elite athletes. Few among us will ever compete at CrossFit Games, putt on the PGA tour, or be trusted to take the game-winning shot in the NBA. But that doesn't mean we're immune to high-pressure situations. Whether you are a recreational tennis player, a Fortune 500 CEO, a painter, or a parent, you will face challenges in critical moments. When they arise, how will you handle them?

"Clutch" is a term thrown around often to describe extraordinary performances in high-pressure situations. Most people associate clutch performances with a triumphant sports moment: the home run that wins the game, the service ace on match point, the basket at the buzzer. But each of these contains an element of luck, and clutch is not luck. Paul Sullivan, in his book *Clutch*, says, "Being clutch is not the hole-in-one to win; it's the well-struck shot close to the flag and the putt that drops in with the tournament on the line. It's the precisely executed series of plays in football, not the Hail Mary pass. It's the fortitude to continue battling out a Wimbledon final as you always have—even though the whole world is wondering whether you are going to choke."

Clutch, simply put, is the ability to do what you can do normally under immense pressure. What Katrín has just done down on the competition floor is extraordinary—not because she pulled an impossible performance out of a hat, but because she was able to deliver her absolute best when everything was on the line. When the stakes were at their highest, she was able to compete exactly the way she trains in the gym, when there are no stakes at all. She focused on the task, not the outcome; she adapted coolly in the face of adversity; she controlled her own performance and ignored her competitors; and she maintained her signature optimistic confidence that if she did everything she could, it would all work out.

It is an exceedingly difficult task. Transferring what you can do in a relaxed atmosphere to a tenser one is not easy; if it were, everyone would be clutch.

So, what's the secret? Why can some people do this and others can't?

You know the answer by now: preparation. If you want to be clutch, you need to strengthen your skills and prepare every day for those high-pressure moments. If you have prepared properly, through training, practice, and ongoing effort, you can rely on that training to help you bring your best. This includes physical training, of course, but just as important is the mental training needed to be great when the stakes are high. The character traits required, the ones that enable my athletes to follow the process, are not developed overnight. For both Mat and Katrín, the gold medals around their necks are the culmination of years of personal development, and only when they approached true mastery did they begin to see results.

It's a lesson everyone can learn from, whether you're an entrepreneur pitching an idea to investors or a recreational golfer trying to improve your game: You cannot summon what you do not have. The traits you need when the stakes are highest—grit, optimism, focus, adaptability, determination, resilience—must be forged in the crucible of training. Who you are on the competition floor is a reflection of who you are in practice—no more, no less.

* * *

For the second year in a row, Katrín is the Fittest on Earth. At the sound of her name, she buries her face in her hands in a mix of elation and relief. She collapses to her knees on the tennis court floor and is overcome with emotion. Tia, in a rousing show of sportsmanship, class, and grace, comes over and hugs her shaking shoulders.

Dave hauls Kat to her feet, then pulls her out to the middle of the floor. She raises both hands over her head and waves at the crowd, which erupts into a festive Viking clap. It starts slow, then builds until the entire tennis stadium is a massive wall of noise. Icelandic flags, which seem to have been procured from thin air, wave from every part of the stadium. Katrín looks around, spots me and O'Keefe in the stands, and abruptly jogs over. She jumps up on a curiously well-placed speaker, and I lean over the railing and give her a hug. I tell her how proud I am of her, how much she deserves it. "Hold on to every minute of this," I tell her. "This is a special moment in your life. Go make some memories." Kat looks at me happily and nods. Then she hops off the step-stool speaker and returns to the floor, a champion once again, and soaks it all in.

EPILOGUE

★

*Vision without action is a dream. Action
without vision is a nightmare.*

—JAPANESE PROVERB

The end of the CrossFit Games always feels a bit surreal,
like Christmas morning after all the presents have been
unwrapped. The staff jokingly refer to it as "CrossFit New
Year," the demarcation of the end of a grueling eight-
month competition season. A low-key awards ceremony
takes place on the floor of the tennis court stadium, during
which the Fittest Man, Woman, and Team are presented
with medals and giant cardboard checks. A hundred boxes
of pizza are also provided, and the athletes leap toward
them like prisoners of war. After the ceremony, most of

the competitors and staff will head back to the Marriott to let loose at the CrossFit-hosted after-party.

Our team is not much for wild parties. Katrín and I skip the after-party in favor of a quiet dinner with our families—we're joined by my wife, Heather, my daughter, Maya, and Katrín's mom and grandpa. Too exhausted to venture far, we end up at McCormick & Schmick's, across the street from the hotel. Predictably, Katrín orders fish and veggies, and she sticks with water. Even in victory, the process reigns.

This book is the story of how well-developed character and unwavering commitment to the process can transform talent into champions. Before I started working with her, Katrín was a middle-of-the-pack CrossFit Games athlete who was content with merely qualifying to compete each year. Mat had been close to winning, but came up short two years in a row. When they committed to the process, everything changed. Katrín won two back-to-back championships, and Mat went from finishing second twice to winning by the largest margin in the history of the CrossFit Games. As I write this, they are the defending Fittest Man and Fittest Woman on Earth.

The strategy outlined in these pages works for the fittest people in the world, and it can work for you. Despite what we're led to believe, greatness is not for the elite few. The mindset of a champion is uncommonly rare, but it doesn't have to be—every one of us is capable of it. Katrín and Mat got to the top of the podium not by virtue of superhuman talent, but through hard work and superior mental qualities. They are living proof that through deep and meaningful practice, anyone can forge and sharpen the mindset of a champion, and use it to improve everything that is important to them.

While writing this book, my athletes, only half-jokingly, implored me not to make it "too good," to not give away our playbook. I always laughed. The truth is that nothing within these pages constitutes a ground-breaking secret, nor represents a particularly innovative new approach. Reading this book will not make you more competitive any more than being an expert in nutrition will get you a six-pack. The only way the process works is through *action*.

Some academic once asked the great Greek orator Demosthenes what the three most important traits of speechmaking were. His reply says it all: "Action, action, action!" While we all have unique circumstances and problems, many change issues come down to the same thing: the ability—or inability—to translate vision into simple, ordinary, everyday actions. That's what the process is about—not some big, hairy, audacious goal, but the thing you can and should be doing today, *right now*, to get there. Katrín and Mat are gifted athletes, but there are many, many gifted athletes. Insofar as there is a secret, this is it: Success is a decision, not a gift. The ideas in this book are only useful insofar as you can *decide* to apply them to your life, consistently, day in and day out.

Jim Afremow, a leading sports psychologist, writes in his book *A Champion's Mind*: "There is no golden road to excellence; excellence is the golden road. Until you start down this road, you'll never have a chance of getting there." In other words, you don't become a champion and then start acting like a champion. Whether you're a professional athlete or a midlevel associate at a law firm, chasing excellence is about living and breathing the behaviors and habits of a champion daily. It's about doing your best at whatever you do, whether it's studying for a test, working out at CrossFit, loading the dishwasher, or listening to a friend in need. It's the manner in which you try to achieve your potential that defines you as a champion, not titles, medals, or accolades. But a curious thing happens when you start acting like a champion—when you commit everything you have to the process, everything else tends to fall into place.

It won't be easy, and it won't happen overnight. You're not going to be perfect; in fact, you're going to struggle a lot along the way. But if you can chase perfection every moment of every day, you can catch excellence. But you have to start.

Go get to work.

ABOUT THE AUTHOR

★

BEN BERGERON has been coaching athletics since 1990, and coaching elite CrossFit Games® athletes since 2009. As the owner of CrossFit New England, his sole professional focus is pursuing a standard of competitive excellence in training. A former competitor himself, he has coached five different CrossFit Games® champions and currently coaches top CrossFit athletes Katrín Davíðs-dóttir, Mat Fraser, Cole Sager, and Brooke Wells. His other great loves are his wife, Heather, and his children.

Printed in Poland
by Amazon Fulfillment
Poland Sp. z o.o., Wrocław